THE ART OF JAPAN

from the Jōmon to the Tokugawa Period

PETER C. SWANN

GREYSTONE PRESS/NEW YORK

Title-page: *'Rain at Shōnō': from 'The Fifty-three Stations of the Tōkaidō'. Wood-block print by Andō (Ichiryūsai) Hiroshige (1797–1858), c. 1833–1840. Private collection.*
Cf. pp. 216, 218.

REVISED EDITION 1966
© HOLLE VERLAG G.M.B.H., BADEN–BADEN, GERMANY
LIBRARY OF CONGRESS CATALOG CARD NUMBER: 66-22128
MANUFACTURED IN THE UNITED STATES OF AMERICA

CONTENTS

LIST OF PLATES

6

LIST OF FIGURES

MAP

ACKNOWLEDGEMENTS

The colour plates on the following pages were kindly supplied by:
Messrs. Benrido, Kyōtō 43, 113, 117, 137, 139, 160, 208
Photo Schmölz, Cologne 166

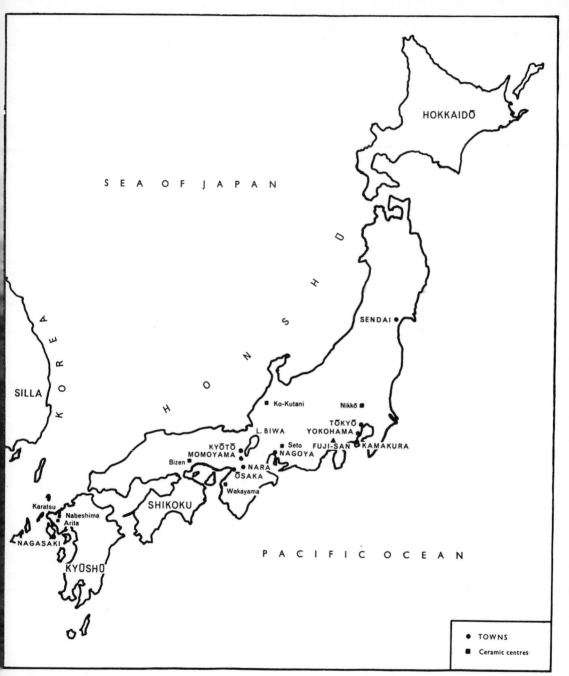

HOKKAIDŌ

S E A   O F   J A P A N

H
O
N
S
H
U

K
O
R
E
A

SILLA

SENDAI ●

■ Ko-Kutani   Nikkō ■

L. BIWA   TŌKYŌ
YOKOHAMA

KYŌTŌ   ▲
MOMOYAMA   ■ Seto   FUJI-SAN ● KAMAKURA
Bizen ■   ● NAGOYA
● NARA
● ŌSAKA

SHIKOKU   ● Wakayama

Karatsu ●
       Nabeshima ■
       Arita
NAGASAKI ●

KYŪSHŪ

P A C I F I C   O C E A N

| ● | TOWNS |
| ■ | Ceramic centres |

JAPAN

I. THE PRE-BUDDHIST PERIOD
(TO THE 6TH CENTURY A.D.)

Geography, climate and geology are powerful factors in moulding *Geographical setting*
the character, and hence the art, of a people. The string of islands,
large and small, which forms the Japanese archipelago stretches in
a long broken arc from a point near the coast of Siberia in the
north to Taiwan in the south. Other smaller chains of islands
link Japan with Korea and the mainland further north. These
routes from north to south and from east to west have never afforded
easy means of communication but they have always been accessible
to the determined traveller or the desperate immigrant.

The isolation of Japan, like that of Great Britain, has played a large
part in shaping her people's outlook over the centuries. Insular to a
degree, the Japanese — unlike the British — were not basically
explorers of the high seas. The urge to colonize came late in their
history.

The four main Japanese islands are Hokkaidō (the North Sea
district), Honshū (the Main Island), Shikoku (the Four Provinces)
and Kyūshū (the Nine Provinces). Altogether there are no less than
five hundred important islands; as a result the country has a relatively long coastline (extending over 17,000 miles) and the sea is
never far away. Sea and shore have always played a major part in
Japanese life and art. In places, especially on the east coast, the
landscape is of unsurpassed beauty. The heart of this romantic coast
is the Inland Sea, whose calm waters are studded with a myriad
green islands of all shapes and sizes.

Through the island chain, from north to south, runs a chain of
volcanic mountains with high peaks worn smooth by the elements.
There are still about fifty active volcanoes scattered throughout the
islands. The mountain passes are comparatively low and communications are not difficult. Dense foliage covers much of the more
high-lying areas and only about one-sixth of the land can be used
for cultivation. This led Sansom to call Japan 'a country that hides

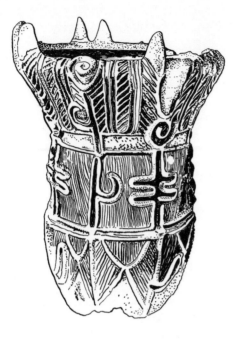

Fig. 1 – *Clay vessel. Mid-Jōmon. Height 61 cm. National Museum, Tokyo. Cf. p. 16.*

poverty behind a smiling face'. Thus the Japanese are accustomed to living in close quarters, a condition which demands attention to the minutiae of human relations and a concern for detail which, again, is reflected in art. The valleys are often narrow and flat with hills rising steeply on either side, giving the landscape a clear-cut sharply defined appearance, with flat areas of colour, that has influenced landscape painting at all times. The land is well watered by rivers and streams, lakes and waterfalls, which add to its beauty — a beauty of which the Japanese are very aware. The climate throughout the island chain varies greatly, but in the main economic areas of Honshū and further south short, hot and humid summers are followed by long, cold but clear winters. The most beautiful periods are spring and autumn, when flowers and trees — which the Japanese greatly admire — deck the land in beauty. Economically life is not easy, for it takes hard work to produce the rice that constitutes the staple crop. Frugality has always been a characteristic virtue of the Japanese people. Stone for building is scarce but wood and bamboo are plentiful; these materials have dictated the architecture and much of the art of Japan, notably its fine early sculpture.

The origins of the Japanese people themselves are very obscure. *Origins* Like Great Britain, Japan forms the furthest extension of a great· land mass with access from north, south and west, so that migrant peoples on reaching Japan could go no further and were forced to merge there. A number of different ethnic elements can be seen in what is now, of course, a well-consolidated population. Man came to Japan quite early but civilization relatively late in the Far Eastern time scale. The earliest arrivals were a Caucasian people from North-east Asia. According to some ethnologists, the remnants of this people — known as the Ainu — still survive in Hokkaidō, where they were driven by more advanced and warlike peoples

FIG. 2 – *Clay figurine. Late Jōmon. Height 17.1 cm. T. Nakazawa Collection. Cf. p. 17.*

13

pressing up from the south. A Manchu-Korean type, a Mongol type and to a lesser degree a Malay type from the Pacific Islands are the three basic elements in the ethnic make-up of modern Japanese man. The Malay element was brought to Japan by the important southwest monsoon from India and the Pacific Ocean and by the warm Kuroshio current which flows northward to Kyūshū. All these ethnological streams have contributed to the artistic outlook of the Japanese.

Shintō The earliest religion of the Japanese people has come to be known as Shintō, or 'the Way of the Gods'. One must, of course, distinguish it from the nationalistic, militaristic Shintōism which was popular in the first half of this century, but even today the older beliefs represent a deep strain in Japanese thought. In its original form it was a primitive animism in which the whole of nature was seen as thronged with spirits and sentient beings. The beauty and fertility of the country make these *kami*, or supernatural spirits, on the whole friendly and gentle; they are bestowers of favours, of food and chil-

FIG. 3 – *Clay vessel. Late Jōmon. Height 42.5 cm. T. Tani Collection. Cf. p. 16.*

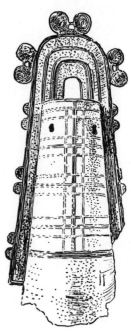

FIG. 4 – *Bronze bell. Late Yayoi. Height 110.5 cm. Metropolitan Museum, New York.Cf. p. 23.* ▶

dren, wealth and longevity, safety and survival, health and happiness. The old religion was a mixture of ancestor worship and nature worship; moral teaching had little part in it. The main ceremony is one of purification which is intended to remove all taint of evil. Purity and simplicity are exalted, images are of no significance. The deepest elements of this belief are still powerful factors and form the basis of some of the most popular new religions.

The earliest culture of which we have any record is known as the *Jōmon culture* Jōmon, 'Cord Pattern' or 'Cord Impression' — so called from its pottery, which is decorated with rich and fantastic cord impressions applied to the outside of vessels. The Jōmon culture was widespread (some 75,000 sites have been recorded) and existed for a very long period, perhaps from as early as the fifth (some say the third)

FIG. 5 – *Rubbing of one of twelve panels on a bronze bell showing hunting scene. H. Hashi Collection. Cf. p. 23.*

FIG. 6 – *Earthenware stemmed cup. Yayoi. Height 15.5 cm., diameter 41.6 cm. National Museum, Tokyo. Cf. p. 24.*

millennium B.C. almost to the Christian era. Towards the end of these centuries the rate of change began to speed up and the elements of a settled way of life began to reach what was originally a nomadic people. The great Bronze Age culture of China which flourished from *c.* 1500 B.C. onwards seems to have made no impact on early Japan.

Jōmon pottery

FIGS. I, 3

The characteristic Jōmon pottery is heavy and built up by hand rather than on a wheel. The clay is unrefined, containing many impurities, and the wares were low-fired. By later ceramic standards and even by those of the Stone Age it is somewhat clumsy, but is distinguished by the variety and fantasy displayed in shape and decoration. It has a sculptural quality, an explosive and restless virility which, strangely enough, has survived in the Japanese taste for ceramics. Whereas the Chinese have always striven for elegance and technical perfection, the Japanese have often been happy in the rough organic feel of the clay and in shapes not dependent on the smoothness and regularity produced by the wheel. The designs are imaginative, highly organized and original. Their barbaric splendour is never overdone or out of balance.

FIG. I

Sometimes (as in Figure I, a mid-Jōmon period pot), the shape is heavy and the decoration a *tour de force* of archaic skill, with the whole surface occupied by irregular but bold patterns. These combine to form a powerful vessel whose inspiration is primitive but far from naive. Figure 3, a late Jōmon piece, is by contrast a slender,

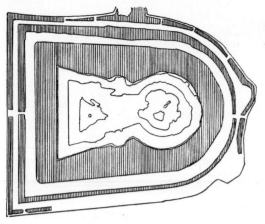

FIG. 7 – *Plan of tomb of Emperor Nintoku (died c. A.D. 400). Cf. p. 25.*

graceful and delicate pot, which might be modelled on a vessel made in another material such as leather. The design of whorls on bands of striations is simple and even elegant in its marked rhythms. A comparison of the two shows the enormous range of artistic sensibility in Japanese Stone Age man. Of all the world's Neolithic pottery, the Japanese Jōmon has the greatest variety and breathes the strongest air of mystery.

Towards the end of the long Stone Age period, but possibly as early as the tenth century B.C., the Jōmon people produced a type of small clay figurine. They are unusually varied in type, some being heavy and as surcharged with detail as the pottery. The exaggerated

PLATES PP. 19, 20
FIG. 2

FIG. 8 – *Stemmed bowl with comb marking. Sue grey ware. Cf. p. 25.*

FIG. 9 – *Gilt bronze helmet. Height 12.7 cm, diameter 22.2 cm. National Museum, Tokyo. Cf. p. 25.*

sexual attributes in many of them suggest that they may belong to fertility cult worship. Others are very lithe, with features which suggest animal forms. The meaning of these figurines remains obscure. It has been suggested that they were substitutes intended to accept the various ills to which mankind is heir. Certainly they have an imaginative power unrivalled in any other culture at a similar stage in man's development. They are most vivid expressions of a spirit-fraught world in which some of the forces have sinister undertones. The work of a highly developed people with strong religious beliefs, they belong to a world of shamanism and witchcraft in which man survives by placating a myriad unseen forces visualized in anthropomorphic or zoomorphic shape.

By the early third century B.C. another people of Mongoloid blood from South China or Indochina reached Japan in considerable numbers by way of Korea. They first occupied northern Kyūshū and during the following six centuries expanded into most of the main island of Honshū, merging with or driving out the earlier inhabitants. The civilization they brought from the mainland (although we do not yet know its exact origin) had been influenced by China and was much more advanced than that of the Jōmon. These Yayoi people (so called from the first site, discovered in Tokyo itself) had an economy based increasingly on agriculture, rice being the main crop. They brought with them a knowledge not only of bronze but also of iron, which from that time onwards was to be used extensively. Japan missed a long Bronze Age and this metal, introduced at a time when in China it was being replaced by

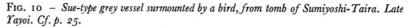

FIG. 10 – *Sue-type grey vessel surmounted by a bird, from tomb of Sumiyoshi-Taira. Late Yayoi. Cf. p. 25.*

PLATE I – Figurine. Late Jōmon. *Height 29.8 cm. National Museum, Tokyo. Cf. p.* 17.

PLATE 2 – Figurine. Mid-Jōmon. *Height 25.7 cm. Y. Yamasaki Collection. Cf. pp. 17.*

PLATE 3 – *Haniwa* figure of woman playing zither *(koto)*. 6th cent. A.D. *Cf. p. 27.*

PLATE 4 – *Haniwa* figures of dancers. 5th-6th cents. *Height of larger figure 34 cm National Museum, Tokyo. Cf. p. 28.*

iron, was employed mainly for ornaments
and artistic objects, such as mirrors, based
on Chinese models. Chinese artistic influences through Korea were very strong,
especially after the establishment of a
Chinese colony in North Korea in 108
B.C., but the Japanese did experiment with
their own bronze designs. The most no-
table are the large bronze bells (*dōtaku*), which are entirely Jap-   FIG. 4
anese in shape and decoration.   *Dōtaku*

These bells are of all sizes, the tallest being about four feet in height.
Starting as very rough products, they reached a high degree of
sophistication. Later examples are most graceful in outline, with a
wide flange that seems almost to bisect the body of the bell. Designs
cast on them vary from the simple and geometric to lively match-
stick designs of human activities such as hunting or cooking. Their   FIG. 5
use seems fairly soon to have been restricted to ritual purposes. The
flaring skirt-like silhouette produced by the wide sweeping flange
gives them a rare elegance, and their beauty is further enhanced by
the bright green patina which many of them have acquired through
burial.

The pottery of the Yayoi culture is quite different from that of the   *Yayoi pottery*
Jōmon people, though at some sites there appears to have been
considerable overlapping. From Korea came knowledge of how to
use the wheel, which gave the pottery regular ceramic shapes and
took away much of the fantasy of the Jōmon. The technique is finer
and the large pots used for coffins must have required great technical

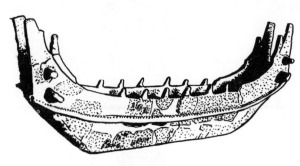

FIG. 12 – *Haniwa model of a boat from Saitobaru tomb, Miyazaki. Length 88.9 cm. National Museum, Tokyo. Cf. p. 27.*

FIG. 6   ability. Figure 6 is a typical Yayoi pot of yellowish red clay, wheel-turned and of elegant stem-cup shape, a shape typical of Far Eastern ceramics. The surface has been smoothed and the general effect is of a well-advanced craft. Often the pots have vigorous painted decorations, frequently of stylized flowers. The colour of the clay is generally reddish and the material much finer than that in the Jōmon.

Korean influence   From the third to the sixth centuries contacts with the mainland, notably with Korea, became much stronger and more intensive than before. On occasions large colonies must have emigrated to Japan, where the knowledge they brought with them was greatly welcomed. During these three centuries a highly organized class system emerged, and guilds of free craftsmen played a considerable part. This

FIG. 13 – *Haniwa model of a building from Saitobaru tomb, Miyazaki. Height 52.7 cm. National Museum, Tokyo. Cf. p. 27.*

period was known as the Old Tomb period from the large number *Old Tomb period*
of tombs — more than ten thousand — located throughout the islands. Figure 7 gives the plan of the largest and most interesting of FIG. 7
these tombs, that of Emperor Nintoku (died *c.* A.D. 400). Occupying
an area of about 80 acres, it rises from the flat plain near Ōsaka and
has remained inviolate over the centuries. This is one notable
example of the Japanese respect for their royal family which has
resulted in the preservation of so much valuable artistic material.
These tombs, often of vast dimensions and surrounded by moats,
have yielded bronze, stone, iron and glass objects of the highest
quality that this period could produce. We reproduce here one of FIG. 9
the most beautiful pieces of armour excavated from a tomb. It is a
gilt bronze helmet made of thin overlapping plates skilfully riveted
to the top central and bottom bands. Mythical animals are lightly
incised on the central band.

During the Old Tomb period another type of pottery was introduced *Sue grey ware*
for use in the tombs; it became widespread throughout Japan by
the sixth century. Technically advanced, of fine non-porous grey FIGS. 8, 10
clay, thinly potted and highly fired, it was obviously a ware made
for the upper classes. Different kinds of combing patterns are used
on varied and interesting shapes. Figure 10, a late example, is a FIG. 10
most elegant stem bowl with a cover decorated with a strong perky
bird. The body and lid show traces of an ash glaze (see below). The
obvious parallel is with similar types in Korea, and Korean potters FIG. 11
must have emigrated in considerable numbers to teach the Japanese
this new type of ware. Comparison between the two makes the
origin of this ware clear beyond all doubt. On some vessels the
shoulders carry animals, somewhat clumsily modelled and by no
means as expressive as the *haniwa* figures. The most significant introduction was that of a rough ash glaze, probably accidental at
first but later skilfully used.

The most striking products of the time, however, are the *haniwa* *Haniwa*
— literally, 'clay circles' — which were implanted into the ground
round the tombs to retain the earth. These red clay models and
figures range from simple well-made pots to complex models and
human figures; they provide fascinating evidence of civilization in PLATES PP. 21, 22

FIG. 14 – *Haniwa figure of warrior in armour. 6th cent.* A.D. *Height 133.1 cm. National Museum, Tokyo. Cf. p. 27.*

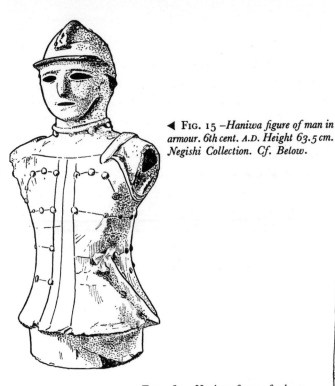

◀ Fig. 15 –*Haniwa figure of man in armour. 6th cent. A.D. Height 63.5 cm. Negishi Collection. Cf. Below.*

Fig. 16 – *Haniwa figure of a horse. 6th cent. Height 83.8 cm. National Museum, Tokyo. Cf. Below.* ▶

Japan just prior to the introduction of Buddhism and Chinese culture. Figure 13 shows the most involved structure depicted in these models, possibly intended to house the soul of the dead. The models show that houses for the first time had boarded sides and independent roofs. Twin-storey buildings seem to have been common. Living conditions had obviously become far more comfortable.

Models of ships and animals, particularly horses, are frequently found. By far the most striking figures are those of the men and women who lived during these three centuries. These models, which date from the beginning of the fifth century A.D. onwards, may have been made quite hurriedly on the death of an important personage; the modelling is rough but most expressive. Warriors in iron and leather armour, huntsmen, and ladies of the court in decorated skirts all reveal a civilization by no means as primitive as was once thought. The plate on page 21 shows a woman of the court with a complicated head-dress, playing a musical instrument, probably a

FIG. 13

FIGS. 12, 16

FIGS. 14, 15
PLATE P. 21

27

kind of zither. The holes for eyes and mouth were possibly a technical consideration to prevent these large models from cracking in the kiln, but this adds greatly to their effect. The modelling, with its economy of means and insistence on essentials, is fresh and spontaneous. PLATE P. 22 taneous. The plate on page 22 represents a group of two dancers who seem to be singing as they dance.

The guilds produced craft works of high quality. Contacts with the mainland must have been very frequent, although the influence of Chinese culture is not yet overwhelming. Living standards, at least for the aristocracy, were high. The sinister atmosphere of the Jōmon has yielded to an optimistic cheerful world in which the gods seem beneficent and man is in control of his destiny.

II. THE ASUKA PERIOD (538–645)

During the early centuries of Japanese history it was considered that the death of an emperor defiled the area in which he lived and for this reason the court moved its location many times. In a relatively unsophisticated society this was comparatively easy, but as the country grew richer and more highly organized such moves of the capital became increasingly difficult and costly. At the beginning of the sixth century the capital was at a place called Asuka — now a small village — in the Nara plain. It was here that Japan's first great cultural revolution took place.

We have already seen that contact with the mainland by way of Korea was always possible, and that it increased considerably between the third and the sixth century A.D. At that time whole colonies of Korean workmen came to Japan, where their superior skills were welcomed by the leaders of the country, who were conscious of the need to modernize. In an atmosphere of political manoeuvre such imported skills represented power. The Chinese script, for instance, was a vital politico-cultural weapon and was introduced at a very early date in Japanese history. The Chinese language not only enabled the Japanese to become literate but also provided the key to an understanding of the whole world of Chinese achievement which the Japanese desired to emulate.

Chinese influence

In the centuries immediately following the fall of the Han dynasty in A.D. 226 China itself was split into a number of warring states. In the turmoil non-Chinese nomadic peoples from the north invaded the country and occupied large areas of the Chinese homeland. Only in the south, where the terrain was unsuited to cavalry warfare and the nomads found the climate unhealthy, were the retreating Chinese able to preserve remnants of their independence and inviolability. To the casual observer it might have seemed that the great days of China's past were gone for ever. The empire was in fragments. The old political and religious systems, once so unassailable, now seemed quite inadequate. The highly organized administrative machinery built up during the Han dynasty had

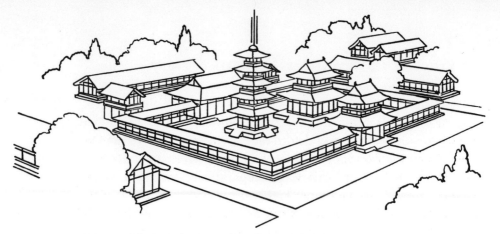

FIG. 17 – *Hōryū-ji Monastery, founded in A.D. 607. Cf. p. 34.*

collapsed and the economy of the country was stricken. Into what most intelligent Chinese must have regarded as political, economic and moral chaos, akin to our 'Dark Ages', came one redeeming force — the Buddhist religion.

Buddhism   This profound and moving faith originated in India in the sixth century B.C. and had slowly been making its way across the inhospitable areas of Central Asia to the Far East. There dissatisfaction with traditional beliefs following the nomad conquests provided fertile ground for its propagation. It spread like fire among a population that clutched at any prospect of an alleviation of their intolerable conditions. Many factors — political, emotional and economic as well as religious — contributed to the rapid success of the faith. The nomadic people who established their kingdoms in North China distrusted the native Confucianism and adopted Buddhism as their official religion. The visual appeal of Buddhist religious paraphernalia, the Buddhas, Bodhisattvas and disciples, the paradises with their occupants appealed to the simple man as much as the subtle philosophy attracted the scholar. The idea that they could retreat to the comparative safety of a monastery in the last resort was congenial to many persons of a reflective turn of mind, while tax relief for the clergy attracted others with less exalted motives.

Under Buddhist inspiration from the fourth century onwards countless Chinese artists produced some of the world's greatest *Cave-temples*   religious art. In the great cave-temples of Tun-huang, Yün-kang and Lung-mên are peerless monuments inspired by religious zeal and artistic skill. The Koreans in turn, through their contact with nomadic peoples in the north of their land, soon learned of the new religion and some may have adopted it as early as the late fourth century. The Japanese, who had long had active contact with the Korean mainland through the state of Paekche (Japanese: Kudara), and for a time even had a physical foothold in the south of the peninsula, learned of it from the Koreans. In this context it must be remembered that Korean scholars went to Japan as early as A.D. 400.

The official date of the introduction of Buddhism into Japan is usually given as A.D. 552, when the ruler of the Korean kingdom of Paekche sent a bronze image of the Buddha and scriptures to the Japanese court. This is only one of the convenient dates on which we like to hang our notions of historical processes that in reality continued over a lengthy period of time.

Buddhism introduced into Japan

Sansom sees the actual adoption of Buddhism as the outcome of a

FIG. 18 – *Large Triad in stone. Yün-kang cave-temples, North China. Northern Wei, A.D. 490–540. Cf. p. 37.*

FIG. 19 – *Buddha seated in niche, in store.*
Yün-kang cave-temples, North China. North-
ern Wei, A.D. 490–540. Cf. p. 37.

political struggle between the conservative forces surrounding the
emperor and the factions pressing for reform. The former were
supporters of the old gods and faiths while the reformers saw in the
Korean system a civilization and organization far more advanced
than their own. Naturally enough they attributed the Koreans'
superiority to Chinese influence. Politically the Chinese system of
centralized administration appealed to the pro-Buddhist faction,
which saw in it a means of controlling unruly local chieftains.
Similarly it could make tax-collecting more effective, and this was
important to a central regime that was attempting the difficult task
of organizing a rapidly expanding nation.

Spread of Buddhism Under the regency of Prince Shōtoku (born 574, died 622), who
ruled on behalf of his aunt, the Empress Suikō, Buddhism was
established almost as a state religion. The Japanese with characteristic thoroughness soon began to by-pass Korea and venture to
the heart of the Buddhist movement in China itself. Missions first
went to the Sui court (the relatively short-lived but impressive
dynasty, 589–618, which preceded the long and splendid T'ang,

32

618–907). Many embassies travelled to the T'ang court itself after the establishment of that dynasty in 618. Such official missions were, of course, important, but they were perhaps not so vital as the many private visits which scholars, priests and craftsmen paid to China. Awe-struck by the spectacle of China in its full power, they brought back glowing reports of the brilliance of the T'ang court, its efficient centralized government of an obedient empire and the wealth which flowed as a consequence. Thus the introduction of Buddhism went hand in hand with the movement towards centralization of the Japanese government. However, unfortunately for subsequent Japanese history, the reformers failed to curb the autonomy of the local chieftains.

The new religion spread rapidly. In Japan the opponents of the faith were not so firmly entrenched as, for example, the Confucians were in China. In this respect it is important to remember that,

FIG. 20 – *Miroku (Maitreya). Korean, from Silla State. Early 7th cent. Duksoo Palace Museum. Cf. p. 44.*

unlike China, Japan suffered no great persecutions of the faith. This was to be of the greatest significance, for many fine early Japanese works of art made under the direct influence of China have survived, whereas in China itself they have disappeared in wars and persecutions. It is a moving experience to be able to see great works of art in highly delicate materials preserved so perfectly for more than a thousand years.

Not only the court but also many great Japanese noble families acted as patrons of the new beliefs. The imposing Hōryū-ji monastery, with its pagoda, lecture hall and surrounding cloisters, was founded as early as A.D. 607 and by A.D. 692 there were no less than 545 monasteries and shrines. The conversion of the Japanese was complete and sincere and, as in the whole of the Far East, Buddhism performed a tremendous service in releasing men's spiritual and artistic imagination.

The Japanese, in taking over Chinese Buddhism, also tried to adopt the Chinese system of state organization, but they sometimes failed

FIG. 21 – *Part of a gilt-bronze banner. Hōryū-ji Monastery, Nara. Overall length 457.5 cm. Cf. p. 47.*

Fig. 22 – *Apsara or flying angel from the front of a niche at Yün-kang. Northern Wei, A.D. 490–540. Cf. p. 48.*

to appreciate the fundamentals on which the Chinese had built the infinitely more advanced nation they were trying to emulate. It is only recently that we in the West have appreciated how impossible it is for one nation to adopt *in toto* the political system of another. Magnificent though the Japanese efforts and achievements were, their lack of understanding led them into certain serious errors which were to have a lasting influence on their later history. The two most far-reaching of these were the position of the monarchy and the foundations on which the civil service was built.

First, over the centuries China had developed the concept that a bad ruler through his misdeeds surrendered his right to rule, his 'Mandate of Heaven', and that the people had the moral right to replace him. This acted as a constant check upon and warning against abuse. The Japanese considered their emperor as a god descended from gods and therefore inviolable. At most periods in

Japanese concept of government

35

FIG. 23 – *Gigaku mask. Wood with metal crown. 28.5 × 20.9 cm. National Museum, Tokyo. Cf. p. 50.*

Japanese history he was little more than a figure-head while ruthless men behind him exercised real power. They could not easily be called to account. The result was that, although the imperial line often survived, the blood-letting, when it did come, was more widespread. Secondly, the Chinese, from the Han dynasty onwards, had developed a system of election to the civil service by examination and in the T'ang centuries this was highly organized and most efficient. Thus, in theory at least, any man through diligence could reach the highest position in the land. However, the Japanese nobility who controlled the destinies of the new nation made higher civil service appointments hereditary in their own ranks. This was a fatal mistake which completely negated the Chinese concept. Japanese public life was thus neither broadly based nor stable.

SCULPTURE
Shaka Triad
In the atmosphere of admiration for China and Korean-Chinese Buddhism it is not surprising that the earliest art should have been dependent on mainland examples. This is immediately visible in

one of the earliest groups, the bronze Shaka Triad in the Hōryū-ji monastery, Nara. (Shaka is Shākyamuni, the historical Buddha.) PLATE P. 39 The statue was made by the *cire-perdue* method; a pious inscription on its back records that a certain Shiba Tori made it in the third month of A.D. 623 in fulfilment of a vow made by the wife of Prince Shōtoku, who had died two years before. Tori's grandfather is said to have come to Japan from Korea in A.D. 522 as a saddle-maker and his experience with bronze horse-trappings must have familiarized him with the problems of working metal.

The type of austere and archaic trinity originated in China during the fifth and sixth centuries in the great cave-temples at such sites as Yün-kang and Lung-mên. The pose is stiff and purely frontal, as FIGS. 18, 19 if it was designed to be seen from the front and high up in a niche on a wall, as they were in the Chinese originals. The main figure of Shaka has the right hand raised in the position intended to dispel fear, while the left is in the position of giving. The figure is an almost perfect pyramid rising from a base of schematized folds which fall like a frozen cascade over the pedestal to the heavy but sensitive face with its 'archaic' smile. The neck is a cylinder which looks clumsy only when considered in isolation. Behind, like an ornate frame setting off the plain lines of the central figure, is a large flame-shaped halo coming to a delicate point at the top, a shape inherited from the stone niche in which the top curved towards the front. With its flames and little seated figures of Buddhas of the Past, this possesses a particular beauty of design and craftsmanship. A number of historians see in this a softness and delicacy which they suggest is a characteristic of Japanese art. The two attendants are almost identical and represent Bodhisattvas, the popular divinities of Mahāyāna (the Greater Vehicle) Buddhism. These are beings who, through their series of good lives, were entitled to enter *nirvāna*, the final release from this world of suffering, but who, from compassion for struggling humanity, elected to stay on earth and help others to achieve the goal. They stand on lotuses which are themselves heavy with Buddhist symbolism. Zimmer summarizes a vast corpus of theory on the importance of the lotus when he says: 'The lotus symbol, as the pedestal of Brahma, acquired in the course of time the meaning of a support for all deities representing the highest transcendental essence....'[1]

Despite the very obvious derivation of this group from mainland traditions, Japanese historians claim that one can indeed see in the elegance and workmanship, in the refinement and sense of pattern, qualities which came to be characteristic of Japanese art. The casting is of a remarkable standard and the detail has a clarity rarely found even in China. The expression on the faces is of deep spirituality, and even in the folds of the robe the sculptor took care to provide just enough variation to avoid deadness. The comparison between the unadorned figure of the Buddha in the centre and the richly ornate attendant figures is most effectively contrived. The manner in which all three are arranged over a small pedestal gives the impression of aerial flight and etherealness.

Kudara Kannon

PLATE P. 40

An even more unusual figure is the Kudara Kannon, also in the Hōryū-ji (Kudara is the Japanese name for the state of Paekche in Korea). It is of wood and in a few places bears traces of lacquer and pigments. Nothing comparable has survived on the mainland either in Korea or in China proper. The style of this very elongated, mysterious divinity is as different as possible from the bronze Shaka Triad with its northern Chinese stone connotations. The direction of the drapery from front to back is most unusual. It has become customary for scholars to assume that this statue reflects influences from the south of China where, following the nomad invasions in the north, the Chinese state of Liang kept Chinese traditions alive. However, we have very little Buddhist statuary from the south in this period and none at all in wood. What has survived would appear to look more to northern styles than to the Kudara Kannon style. The peculiar elongation recalls many Wei dynasty tomb figurines. It is assumed that the figure was either brought from Korea or made in Japan by a Korean immigrant. If one can draw any parallels, one can say that the treatment of the drapery in broad flat bands is reminiscent of marble sculpture of the Chinese Sui period (A.D.

[1] H. R. Zimmer, *The Art of Indian Asia* (New York 1955), pp. 158–230.

PLATE 5 – Shaka Triad. Gilt bronze. Hōryū-ji Monastery, Nara. *Height of seated figure 86.4 cm. Cf. p. 37.*

PLATE 6 – Kudara Kannon. Wood. Hōryū-ji Monastery, Nara. *Height 209.7 cm. Cf. p. 38.*

PLATE 7 – Miroku (Maitreya). Wood. Kōryū-ji Temple, Kyōtō. *Height 124.5 cm. Cf. p. 47.*

PLATE 8 – Detail of panel on the Tamamushi shrine. Lacquer on wood. Hōryū-ji Temple, Nara. *64.8 × 35.6 cm. Cf. pp. 50. 131. 145.*

PLATE 9 – The Gakkō Bosatsu ('Moonlight Bodhisattva'). One of the attendants of the main Yakushi Buddha (Buddha of Healing) in the Yakushi-ji Temple, Nara. *C.* A.D. 720. *Cf. p. 60.*

PLATE 10 – Large clay figure of the Nikkō Bosatsu ('Sunlight Bodhisattva'). Late Nara. Tōdai-ji Temple, Nara. *Height 179.2 cm. Cf. p. 62.*

PLATE 11 – Portrait of the Priest Ganjin. Hollow dry lacquer. Late Nara. *Height 80.1 cm.*
Cf. pp. 72, 123.

45

PLATE 12 – Section of the *E-Ingakyō* ('Illustrated Sūtra of Causes and Effects in the Past and Present') showing the daughters of the King of Evil attacking the Buddha. Ink and colour on paper. 8th cent. *Height 26.7 cm. Cf. p. 73*

589–618), the short period which united China and led to the long T'ang dynasty.

Despite its seeming naiveté of inspiration and simplicity of design this Bodhisattva of Compassion is a most sophisticated statue. An air of mystic devotion gives it a kind of transcendental calm and remoteness that distinguishes it completely from the other major works of the period that have survived.

The earliest examples of Buddhist sculpture in this period show as much diversity as they do fervour and intensity. Outstanding for its pure elegance and grace is the Miroku (Sanskrit: Maitreya) or 'Buddha of the Future', now in the Kōryū-ji, Kyōtō. It is less than life-sized and made from a single piece of broad-grained red pine wood, unlike other early wood sculptures which are of camphor wood. Although once probably covered with lacquer, the wood is now bare and with its exposed grain contributes to the elegant flow of the carving, especially in the sweep round the cheeks. The model for this highly evocative work is plainly Korean, as is shown by the bronze statue in the National Collection in Korea. The lissom grace and benevolent aspect reflect an unsophisticated adoration, a religious atmosphere as yet uncoloured by the darker tones of later Buddhist thought. It is sculpted far more in the round than the Tori bronze and in a sense represents with a new confidence the divine brought down to earth. As with most early images, the gaze is turned inwards towards its own gentle spiritual world but it has a unique modesty and shyness.

Miroku

PLATE P. 41

FIG. 20

None of these statues, made at a time when Japan was enthralled by the example of her great neighbours, gives an opportunity to judge the real artistic characteristics of the Japanese. They only show how much a nation can do, given faith and determination. Such outward lasting qualities persist throughout Japanese history and account for the basic ambivalence in the nation's culture.

The Tori Triad and Kudara Kannon are only two of the many treasures of early Japanese art in the Hōryū-ji. One of the earliest examples of Buddhist metalwork is the gilt-bronze banner in Figure 21. The whole banner is over fifteen feet in length and filled with a fine flowing design of cut-out figures surrounded by an ara-

FIG. 21

besque border. On one side only the figures are incised. The whole surface is covered with Buddhist figures, in particular with floating *apsaras*, heavenly beings who play musical instruments or make offerings to the Buddhas in the various paradises. The origin of these figures is, of course, again China and pre-T'ang. One finds countless similar figures on the ceilings and round the niches of the cave-temples. Belief in the existence of such beautiful occupants of heaven was an inducement for the simple to believe in the bliss of the Buddhist hereafter. The origins of this belief may well go back to one of the *Jātaka* tales, or stories from the previous lives of the Buddha. In one of these, for example, it is told how the Buddha converted a man particularly fond of the pleasures of the flesh by showing him a vision of paradise in which the denizens were far more beautiful than those to whom he was attached on earth. The free flowing design within a formal border is most effective and the silhouette technique goes right back to Chinese Han dynasty times. The sense of movement, of life, was by now one of the prime requirements of painting and the Japanese have here most effectively translated it into metal. If the central deities, in particular the Buddha figures, were of necessity calm and unadorned, physically beyond the wit of man, craftsmen could exercise their skill and love of movement in these attendant figures, who swarm around in adoration much as the living worshippers of the time must have done. The skill in expression of drapery is conveyed in every medium with consummate ease — a quality which is shared by the Chinese. The Japanese throughout their art have always shown a particular interest in facial characteristics. This has produced some of the finest portraiture in the Far Fast. It has also led to an interest in the grotesque aspects of the human face. The masks for which the Japanese are famous were used in stage performances or in religious dances and ceremonies. The major Buddhist figures tend to fall into somewhat set types, which do indeed change, but only somewhat slowly. This is due to the belief that for religious efficacy the Buddha

FIG. 22

MASKS

FIG. 24 – *Tamamushi shrine. Hōryū-ji Temple, Nara. Cf. p. 50* ▶

48

figures should correspond to certain fixed canons of size and physical characteristics. Only thus would they embody the religious magic of their originals. In the masks the fantasy of the carvers was given free rein. The dances for which such masks were used were performed at large temples and shrines in formal rituals in imitation of those of the more culturally advanced nations on the continent.

FIG. 23 The impressive music for which the Gigaku mask in Figure 23 was made probably originated in China and has survived in Korea and Japan. It is possible that similar masks were used there but none have survived; nor are they represented in other arts of the mainland. This had led some historians to suggest that the Japanese love of masks is a characteristic inherited from the Pacific peoples rather than from mainland Asia, and that in this respect the Japanese reveal traces of their southern blood.

Certainly, in such masks, which often come close to caricature, the Japanese show a sense of humour which is un-Chinese. The Chinese are a humorous people in their daily life but humour seldom appears in their art. With the Japanese the reverse is true. Again the Japanese frequently push their interests to an extreme, as if, having learned something, they are determined to explore it more deeply than their teachers.

PAINTING IN LACQUER To the Asuka period also belong the earliest examples of Japanese painting to have survived. These are the paintings in lacquer on the Tamamushi or 'Beetle-wing' shrine which is also preserved in the PLATE P. 42 treasury of the Hōryū-ji. The name comes from the beetles' wings which were placed beneath the open metalwork of frames and FIG. 24 borders and which reflected with a dull purple gleam any light that fell upon them. The most famous of these panels again illustrates a *Jātaka* story. This tells how one day the Buddha in a former life was walking in the country. He happened to come upon a starving tigress with her young and, out of compassion for all living creatures, gave his life to feed them.

The various parts of this drama — the Buddha's disrobing, his plunge downwards into the lair and his final sacrifice are all shown in the same picture as three scenes superimposed on the same background — a technique often used in early Buddhist art both in

50

China and Japan. This technique is found in *Jātaka* paintings on the walls of the cave-temple site of Tun-huang in the far west of China. The interesting landscape conventions seen here have a long history which goes back to Han and even pre-Han times, while the flat spatula-type rocks derive from Indian models.[1] Certainly they appear in China in pre-T'ang times; the most famous

[1] Cf. M. Sullivan, *The Birth of Landscape Painting in China* (London 1962), pp. 129-31.

FIG. 25 – *Side of an engraved stone sarcophagus, c. A.D. 525. Nelson Gallery of Art, Kansas City. Cf. p. 52.*

FIG. 25 example is, of course, the well-known late sixth-century sarcophagus in the Kansas City Museum. There a similar type of rock occurs but the foliage is of a more complicated and developed style. The Tamamushi bamboos are very naturalistic but the schematized rocks and naturalistic foliage in no way conflict. The figures play out their drama with calm and determined assurance. The slender figure of the Buddha in his simple white dress acts as a perfect foil to the richly adorned figures of Bodhisattvas painted on other panels.

We see here the easternmost extension of Chinese theories on the art of painting with which Japanese craftsmen must have become familiar on their visits to China. As early as the fifth century the most famous of the early theorists, Hsieh Ho, had emphasized the need for an artist to give his work the 'life breath' and thereby create a sense of movement. The Japanese achieved this with great effect while still giving the whole vision the delicacy and soft intimacy which characterize their approach to art. It is interesting to note in passing that Far Eastern painting is almost invariably in ink or water-colour. Oil painting does not exist; for the most usual type of scroll, which could be rolled up and stored away conveniently, oils would have been quite useless. However, in lacquer the Japanese (and also the Koreans) came near to Western techniques. Even judged by Western standards of oil painting, these panels are remarkable achievements for their time.

The art of the Asuka period was produced not by mystics but in that atmosphere of admiration and wonder which is the essence of true religion and great religious art. Faced with what they considered a higher ideal, the Japanese exerted all their energies to its attainment with the single-mindedness for which they have become famous. Totally committed, they accepted whatever came to them without question. Never again was their Buddhist art to be so unaffected and uncomplicated. With deeper insight came difficulties which brought out the inherent characteristics of their art.

III. THE NARA PERIOD (710–784)

The Japanese visitors to China experienced for the first time the sight of the grand capital city of a mighty empire — wealthy, far-flung and highly organized. Ch'ang-an, the Chinese capital under the T'ang dynasty (618–907), seethed with cosmopolitan life. Great poets and painters enlivened its atmosphere. Religious tolerance and intellectual curiosity were its hallmarks, at least in the eighth century. Foreigners of many colours and creeds thronged its streets, providing a touch of the exotic. Grand palaces, fine temples and a vast complex of administrative buildings provided an imposing centre for the city, while the lesser dwellings of ordinary citizens, their noisy shops and markets, restaurants and entertainment quarters crowded around them as far as the eye could see. Nothing remotely comparable existed in Japan. The grandeur of Ch'ang-an inspired the Japanese with a desire to emulate the Chinese example. They sent embassies which sometimes numbered as many as five hundred men, who were bent on learning all they could of its marvels in the shortest time possible. *Ch'ang-an*

Yet while Ch'ang-an alone contained about two million citizens, it must be remembered that the entire population of Japan at the time was only about six million and that the resources of the islands were only a fraction of those of China. However, with a high sense of urgency and the utmost seriousness the Japanese set about creating a miniature China.

The principal result was Nara, a Chinese-style city. It measured 2¾ by 3 miles in area (about one-quarter the size of Ch'ang-an) and was laid out in A.D. 710 on the regular grid pattern typical of Chinese cities. Even today, when the tide of government has passed it by for more than a thousand years, enough remains of its old temples and parks, preserved with the care for which the Japanese are well known, to recall vividly the atmosphere of a T'ang dynasty city. It was here, in these grand architectural surroundings, that *Nara*

FIG. 26 – *Design on one of the lotus-leaves forming the base of the Great Buddha, Tōdai-ji Temple, Nara. Late Nara period. Cf. p. 58.*

Japan settled down for the first time to the serious study and assimilation of the new Chinese culture — its language, literature, religion, philosophy, administration and art. It is difficult to understand how the effort that this required did not ruin them. In the arts and crafts offices were established under the Household Department or the Treasury to supervise the production of paintings, bronzecastings, lacquer ware, woven textiles etc., both for current use and to encourage and train craftsmen. So well did they learn their lesson that it is often difficult even for experts to distinguish between pieces made in China and those made a few years later in Japan. With the study of Buddhism came a deeper insight into the philosophy, ethics and metaphysics of the Indian faith which had swept through China. With this deeper knowledge came also the sectarianism which study inevitably seems to breed. Of the new early sects the Hossō and Ritsu were the most important. Abuses

Development of Buddhism

54

also crept in. Tax-free lands given to the proliferating monasteries curtailed the central revenue; Japan was neither rich nor large enough to support this luxury. As the priesthood gained in wealth and influence so also it began to interfere actively in politics. The most infamous example of this was the priest Dōkyō, a Japanese Rasputin, who became the lover of an empress and about A.D. 770 launched a scheme, which was nearly successful, to have himself made emperor. The economic advantages to be gained by entering a monastery attracted a number of men who were debarred by birth from high civil office but were otherwise unsuited to religious life. They saw the church as a safe and speedy means of achieving wealth and power. They constituted a parasitic element which vitiated many a well-intentioned scheme.

The extensive literature of China acted as a model for the Japanese. The first history of Japan, the *Kojiki* or 'Record of Ancient Matters', was completed in 712. Confucianism also came to Japan at this time, *Confucianism* although it was to have far less influence on Japanese life than Buddhism. The two Confucian concepts which the Japanese could

FIG. 27 – *The Shōsō-in at Nara. Cf. p. 58.*

readily appreciate were filial piety and ancestor worship. Both had affinities with Japanese thought of the period. Although the dry moralizing of Confucian practice might appeal to the Sinicizing scholar or to the ruling class in Japan, it meant little to the common man, whose imagination was fired by Buddhism.

The ambitions of the Japanese to establish a nation organized on Chinese lines inevitably met with only limited success. The central government organs seem to have been fairly effective but the local government system which effectively held China together did not develop in Japan, where there were no other towns of any size to act as local centres. An organized mercantile system, which might have acted as a unifying agent, was equally lacking in Japan at this time.

Social life   Although noble and priest enjoyed relatively easy lives, the people were less fortunate. The *corvée* and forced labour were probably the most hated of all the exactions imposed upon the farming community. In addition the farmers were impoverished by the demands made on them to help build the new capital. Two alternatives faced them. Either they could become semi-slaves working on the lands of the temples or large landowners or, driven by hunger or oppression, they could turn to robbery. Throughout the period armed bands roaming the relatively undeveloped countryside were a constant danger. Langdon Warner gives a vivid picture of life during the Nara period in his book, *The Enduring Art of Japan*.[1]

SCULPTURE   Both the megalomania among the rulers of Nara and the religious fervour among the people of the period are typified by the decision

Great Buddha   to cast a huge bronze figure 53 feet high in the Tōdai-ji Temple at Nara. This 'Great Eastern Temple' had become the headquarters of the Kegon sect, which reached Japan in 736. Its teaching centred on the worship of the Vairocana (Japanese: Rōshana) Buddha, the Universal Buddha of whom all the other Buddhas, including Shākyamuni, the historical Buddha himself, were only

[1] Harvard, 1952.

56

manifestations. The temple became a religious centre of great power and was certainly the most important one during the period; its influence reached out to its subordinate temples in the provinces. A smallpox epidemic of 735 inspired Emperor Shōmu to set up this great monument and in 749, after a number of failures, the figure was finally completed. About one million pounds of metal were used in casting it; almost miraculously, as if by divine intervention, a gold mine was found in a remote province which yielded 500 lbs. of gold, and enabled the casters to gild the statue. This discovery was an occasion for nation-wide rejoicing. The building constructed to house this colossus was 284 feet long, 166 feet wide and 152 feet high — the largest wooden structure ever built. It burned down in the twelfth century and the present building, although only two-thirds the size of the original, is still the largest wooden building under a single roof in the world. The original statue has unfortunately also been damaged by fire and subsequently most clumsily repaired. Thus, apart from its great size, it is undistinguished. Only a few of the original lotus petals which decorate the base

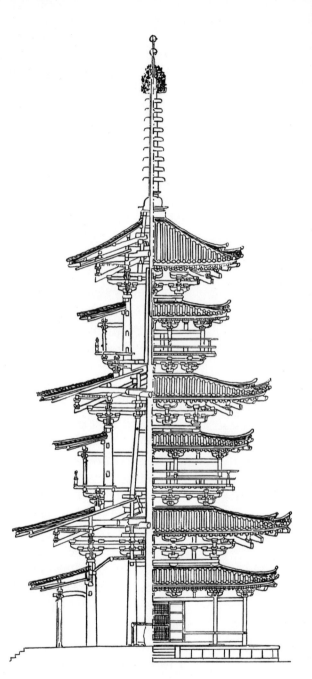

FIG. 28 – *East Pagoda of the Yakushi-ji Temple, Nara. 8th cent. Cf. p. 59.*

FIG. 26 remain; some of these have incised figures whose grace and artistry match that of the inspired originals.

The emperor dedicated the statue in 752 with an eye-touching ceremony of great solemnity and splendour, intended to impart life to the figure. The enthusiasm for the new faith, of which this was the most outstanding illustration, shows that Buddhism had by now become in effect a national religion. The Shintō beliefs of the ancients seemed for a while to be in eclipse, or, to be more accurate, assimilated into the new religion. Nevertheless, the Japanese were always careful to pay lip-service and some genuine respect to the old gods. In the centuries to come Shintō beliefs were to show themselves most resilient.

The building of the hall and the Great Buddha shows how effective the Japanese were in building up a corpus of artisans skilled in all the arts and crafts. This vitality, which seems to work best under emotional stimulus, is characteristic of the race at all periods. Refugees from Korea still flocked to Japan, especially after the fall of the Korean kingdoms of Paekche and Kōguryō (i.e. Kudara and Kōkuri); the grandfather of the man who supervised the casting of the Great Buddha was one of these refugees. But within two generations the Japanese were masters of the basic crafts. They might take inspiration from China but they were fully capable of imposing their own artistic personality on what they chose.

Shōsō-in

FIG. 27

FIG. 31

Yet another example of court support for Buddhism is provided by the Shōsō-in. In A.D. 756 the empress gave the entire household equipment of her recently deceased husband to the Tōdai-ji Temple in Nara. This huge collection, comprising nearly 10,000 objects, ranging from weapons and furniture to textiles and pottery, was installed in a huge log cabin set up on stilts. This, the oldest 'museum' in the world, remained untouched through the centuries, preserved only by respect for the imperial household and by the seals on its great doors. Until recently it was opened once a year in autumn for the traditional airing, but more recently a selection of its treasures has been on show in the National Museum, Nara, while the remainder are constantly being cared for and catalogued. Although most of the objects it contains are of Chinese manufacture and of a quality suitable for royal use, a number of them are made by Japanese in emulation of Chinese prototypes. Among them are some examples of pottery and some painted screens (see page 71).

The first part of the Nara period, i.e. from 645 to 712, is sometimes *Hakuhō period* known as the Hakuhō period from the most important sub-period within it (A.D. 672–86). Artistically speaking, the period was a continuation and intensification of the Asuka period with the more unified direction of T'ang art and the refinements which improved techniques brought. The sculptors were still under the influence of early spiritual exaltation, and tended to humanize their figures. However, they were not as yet able to impose their own characteristics on the Buddhist art they had inherited. Much effort went into the erection of religious buildings, and some 500 had been built by the end of the century; of these the most outstanding example to have survived is the pagoda of the Yakushi-ji, dating to 718, with its graceful proportions and complicated bracketing system. Chinese influences from as early as the Sui period (589–618, i.e. just before the T'ang) begin to appear in bronze statues such as the Shō Kannon in the Kakurin-ji Temple.

Japanese contacts with China proper brought the country into close touch with a cosmopolitan world in which China in its turn was strongly under the influence of the west. In many ways art under the T'ang dynasty was the least purely Chinese period in the whole of her history. Influence

FIG. 29 – *Clay figure of a girl. East side of the group on the ground floor of the Five-storeyed Pagoda of the Hōryū-ji Temple, Nara. A.D. 711. Cf. p. 61.*

came from north-west India, i.e. the Gandhāra area, where pure Indian styles had merged with those of the Roman Empire. In India itself the attractive sensual art of the Gupta period at its height (*c.* 375–490) made a strong appeal to the T'ang Chinese. In Central Asia, at oases like Khotan, Karashar, Kuchā and Kashgar, stepping-stones on the journey of the faith from India to China, artists were developing styles in which Iranian influences also played their part. Thus the art of China which the Japanese so admired and adopted was itself the mature synthesis of a number of different artistic streams brought by different routes, some directly, some less directly, and then re-interpreted by the Chinese. For the first time Japanese art, following powerful Chinese influences, begins to have a unified style.

Gakkō Bosatsu

PLATE P. 43

The Chinese T'ang dynasty traditions of monumentality, dignity and warm living qualities are represented at their finest in the Gakkō Bosatsu ('Moonlight Bodhisattva'). This is one figure of a trinity and one of the companion figures to the main seated Buddha in the Yakushi-ji, the Temple of the Buddha of Healing in Nara. Made of gilt bronze (the gilding has now gone) in about 720, it has been called the finest T'ang statue to have survived. Comparable figures in China have long since been melted down for their metal or destroyed in wars and persecutions of the faith. The technique of casting is unsurpassed.

The figure, which is more than life-size, is completely relaxed, with the hips seductively bent. The whole body sways in the Indian *tribhanga* or 'thrice-bent' pose. The majesty of T'ang and the Indian appreciation of physical attributes are here perfectly combined. Thin floating drapery reveals a body of warm living flesh, expressed without any of the reticence which generally accompanies the Chinese interpretation of the unclothed human figure. Yet although human characteristics dominate the period, behind them lies a powerful spirituality rooted in the conviction of the unity of the worlds of God and man. Every gesture is highly disciplined; despite their obvious bodily charms they remain very much gods, the embodiment in human form of deep spiritual forces.

By the time T'ang art was introduced into Japan, the Chinese had

behind them nearly a thousand years of experience in the modelling
of clay figures for the tomb. Many are little masterpieces of careful
observation which rise above the mass-production methods used in
their manufacture. During the T'ang dynasty the Chinese added to
their mastery of naturalistic representation a great sense of movement and a curiosity about the anatomical variety they saw around
them. The Japanese themselves produced some such small clay FIG. 29
figures, which have a more personal, individual cast of feature than
the mass-produced Chinese examples. In the ground floor of the
Five-storeyed Pagoda of the Hōryū-ji is a small square dais of clay,
in its centre an interpretation of Mount Sumeru (the cosmic mountain of Indian thought) with cave-
like hollows on all four sides. Each
cave has a group of statuettes arranged in tableau form. The temple records state that the whole
model was placed there in 711.
One side has a *nirvāna* scene in
which Shākyamuni, the historical
Buddha, is surrounded by heavenly beings, the Ten Great Disciples, the Eight Guardian Monks,
nuns, worshippers, birds and animals, etc. — even a doctor who
seems to be watching the dying
Buddha's pulse. Like the larger
statues they are of rough clay,
covered with fine clay and then a
coating of kaolin, which was originally painted. The sense of drama
is matched only by some of the
Tun-huang groups. Here in miniature are the cave-temples of

FIG. 30 – *Clay figure of a Bodhisattva from
Tun-huang. 8th cent. Fogg Art Museum,
Cambridge, Mass. Cf. p. 62.*

China, but the personalization of the figures is an essentially Japanese feature.

Such figures were originally of small scale but from about the fourth century onwards the Chinese started to produce clay figures in life-size. Such sites as Tun-huang in the far west, where good natural stone for carving did not exist, forced the Buddhist worshipper to produce large statues in clay. It is probable that they also produced them for the temples but their fragility generally led to their destruction and as a result the Japanese examples are the finest to have survived. That they remain in all their crispness of manufacture, though most of the paint has dropped off, is almost incredible. They are made on a rough core or framework of wood. This is in turn covered with coarse clay mixed with straw, followed by a finer layer of clay and mica dust. The whole figure was then painted and embellished with gold leaf.

The so-called Nikkō Bosatsu ('Sunlight Bodhisattva') in the Tōdai-ji at Nara is one of the most outstanding of these early clay figures. It is incorrectly named, for in fact it is intended to represent a Ten or Deva, a heavenly being as opposed to an earthly being or one from hell. This is one of a number of Hindu deities which were incorporated into the Buddhist pantheon at a very early date and which the natives of the Far East took over without understanding their origin. Such figures reveal the essence of Nara period art. Both monumental and spiritual, they present a picture of Buddhism as a straightforward uncomplicated vision in which the faith is basically a benevolent, sympathetic expression of the human spirit. At the same time it reflects, in restrained tones, the wealth and elegance demanded by an opulent Chinese taste. This is shown in an interest in complicated adornments, haloes, jewellery, flowing robes and elegant hair-styles. However, the artists resisted any temptation they may have felt to indulge in iconographical *tours de force*.

The late Nara period is sometimes called the Tempyō period from its most important years (729–48); many critics consider its sculptural work the finest which Japan has produced. The period is marked by tremendous zeal and prolific output in all kinds of material and techniques. Its qualities are great solemnity, sincerity

FIG. 30

Nikkō Bosatsu

PLATE P. 44

Tempyō period

62

PLATE 13 – Kichijō-ten ('Goddess of Good Fortune'). Ink and colour on hemp. 8th cent. Yakushi-ji Temple, Nara. *Cf. pp. 74, 97.*

PLATE 14 – Wall-painting of a Bodhisattva from the walls of the Kondō (Main Hall) of the Hōryū-ji, Nara, now destroyed. *Cf. pp.* 75, 77.

PLATE 15 – Yakushi Nyōrai (Buddha of Healing). Wooden figure in the Gangō-ji Temple, Nara. *Height 144.8 cm. Cf. p. 82.*

PLATE 16 – Nyōirin Kannon ('The Goddess of Compassion with the Gem and Wheel which Satisfy All Desires'). Painted wooden statue in the Kanshin-ji Temple, Ōsaka. *Height 109 cm. Cf. p. 84.*

PLATE 17 – Aka ('Red') Fudō. Colour on silk. Myōō-in, Mount Kōya, Wakayama Prefecture. ▶ *165.2 × 95.9 cm. Cf. p. 95.*

PLATE 18 – Amida by Jōchō. Gilded wood. Byōdō-in, Uji near Kyōtō. *Height 284.7 cm. Cf. p. 102.*

PLATE 19 – Kichijō-ten. Painted wood. Jōruri-ji Temple, Kyōtō. *Height 90.2 cm. Cf. p. 103.*

PLATE 20 – Amida Raigō (detail). The Buddha Amida descending to the world. Colour on silk. Anon-ymous. Late 11th cent. Daien-in, Mount Kōya, Wakayama Prefecture. *Overall size 210.9 × 419.4 cm.* *Cf. p. 104.*

and conviction. In the many noble works of the period the Japanese show their fine feeling for surface and texture and their skill in interpreting the gentle rhythms of drapery. Later this gentleness sometimes led them into sweet sentimentality, but these inherent tendencies are here balanced by the nobility of the fundamental concept. The very human quality of the statues is ensured by the sensitive attention to facial characteristics and to hands, drapery and hair. The gentle expression is thrown into clear relief by the heavy shoulders and chest. No sexual characteristics are suggested. But the intimacy, the sense of human divinity, the portraiture is unique in the Far East to the artistic genius of Japan.

This attention to attributes of personality, which distinguishes so much early Japanese art, reveals a society in which the individual was important. Japan has always admired the power of the individual, and in a small, fairly intimate society such as that of early Japan the accretion of power and influence in a few hands was relatively early. The history of the conversion of Japan to Buddhism abounds in stories of the achievements of intrepid seekers after the truth, of the exploits of Chinese missionaries bringing new sects and of Japanese converts seeking instruction in China. The self-sacrificing lives of the early Buddhist teachers contain passages as inspiring as those in the history of early Christianity.

FIG. 31 – *Portrait of a woman. Detail for a screen in ink and slight colour on paper. Early 8th cent. Shōsō-in, Nara. 125.8 × 66.1 cm. Cf. p. 58.*

Fortunately the Japanese have left portraits of some of these men — warm human documents which reveal the emotional, personal, and at times even sentimental side of the Japanese character. One of the earliest and most moving of these early portraits is a statue of the monk Ganjin, a Chinese missionary who came to Japan in 753 at the invitation of the Emperor Shōmu. In the course of six attempts to reach the islands he lost his eyesight but lived to found the Tōshōdai-ji, where this tribute to him is housed. Ganjin died in 763, and the statue was made a few years after his death by an artist who is said to have been Ganjin's own pupil.

The technique used for this figure is known as dry lacquer. Lacquer is the sap of a tree which Eastern people have always valued highly and used for decorative purposes — mainly for making utensils such as cups, bowls and ladles, boxes, trays and furniture. Sculptors sometimes used it as a thick top coating over a rougher wooden core in which they made the final modelling. Sometimes they used hemp impregnated with lacquer, which was formed over a light wooden frame and the whole rough form then covered with more layers of lacquer in which the surface modelling was carried out. The process originated in China and some T'ang dynasty examples have survived, but in relatively poor condition. The technique, though difficult, has advantages in that figures made of lacquer are light and easily transportable, especially in procession, and also in that they are impervious to the destructive activity of insects. But such statues cannot of course survive rough treatment and they tend to crack in extremely dry climates. When the Japanese explored fully the possibilities of wood-carving, in which their true genius lay, they abandoned lacquer as a material for sculpture. The Ganjin portrait shows the full possibilities of dry lacquer for sensitive modelling and soft effects. The lacquer smoothes out the sharpness between drapery and body and creates an impression of smooth lines and texture. The sculptor has skilfully drawn attention to the delicate features with their poignant expression — the gentle

FIG. 32 – *Typical example of the plump type of Chinese T'ang tomb figurine, representing a lady of the court. Cf. p. 75.*

but firm mouth, the sightless eyes (this is not just an eyeless statue) and the inward-looking expression of a man who has achieved inner peace. The statue breathes a radiance and serenity which raise it to the highest level of devotional art. A simple monastic robe covers the prelate's thin body; his hands rest in his lap, palms turned upward in the *mudrā* of concentration, 'the gesture which indicates the suppression of all spiritual disquiet in order to arrive fully at complete concentration on the truth'; the mouth has the slightly drawn quality of pain overcome and of inner triumph. No comparable document of the religious spirit in human form exists in China.

To turn from sculpture to painting, one finds that the art of Nara is still dominated by Buddhism and its appeal to the visual imagination. The Chinese Buddhist scriptures were inaccessible to all but scholars trained in continental culture, and these were relatively few in number. Yet at the same time the need to carry the message to the uneducated was felt strongly and the evangelists developed a simple pictorial method whereby the most obvious aspects of the faith could be expressed in straightforward terms. The *E-Ingakyō* or 'Illustrated Sūtra of Causes and Effects in the Past and Present', from this period, has survived in part. This is a Buddhist scripture in four volumes, translated into Chinese by an Indian priest named Gunabhadra. It originally comprised a series of continuous paintings which illustrate the text written beneath them. The technique is quite unpretentious, the stage being set with a minimum of aids — a few trees and rocks to suggest the rolling countryside, a simple structure to show a palace.

The story illustrated here is one of the most famous in Buddhist lore. It depicts the last act of the Buddha's search for truth. Having tried by various methods to reach the truth and failed, he went out into the wilderness and sat for one night in contemplation under the Bodhi Tree. During this period he underwent a number of trials, one of which was temptation by the three daughters of Māra, the King of Evil, who appeared to him in the guise of beautiful women. This he successfully resisted and after more temptations and attacks, as dawn broke, he achieved enlightenment and became

PAINTING

E-Ingakyō
PLATE P. 46

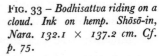

Fig. 33 – *Bodhisattva riding on a cloud. Ink on hemp. Shōsō-in, Nara. 132.1 × 137.2 cm. Cf. p. 75.*

the Buddha, the Enlightened One.

Such simple and unpretentious paintings are probably the products of a temple painting office which created them in quantity. The colours are strong and the lines bold. The skill in telling a continuous story anticipates the achievements of the painted hand-scrolls of the Fujiwara and Kamakura periods (see below). The simplified land-scape conventions are those developed in China and seen in all the early pastoral painting that came from Central Asia through China. The appeal of its humour and charming directness survives the centuries.

Painting in the early Nara period, like sculpture, was strongly in-fluenced by China's example. The best illustration of this is the famous Kichijō-ten in the Yakushi-ji at Nara. This small painting of the Goddess of Good Fortune is painted in graded colouring on hemp. The jewelled head-dress and sacred jewel in her left hand are symbols of her miraculous powers. The dress is richly decorated, green and pink colours predominating.

Kichijō-ten in Yakushi-ji

PLATE P. 63

The type of feminine beauty shown here is taken directly from the T'ang court ideal of feminine beauty — plump and matronly with rounded cheeks, small mouth and shaped eyebrows. The type is

74

said to originate from a certain famous courtesan, Yang Kuei-fei, of Turkish origin, the mistress of Emperor Ming Huang (713–55). She was rather plump by Chinese standards of feminine beauty, but all the court ladies were compelled to follow the modes she established. Many Chinese tomb figurines have survived which show similar, rather un-Chinese forms. The matronly look is perhaps FIG. 32 suitable for a goddess who is supposed to provide good fortune. The figure, with its human tones, voluptuous body and highly made-up face, is certainly secular in outlook and illustrates how the Nara period was impressed by the glamour of T'ang civilization.

A similar feeling is seen in the seated Bodhisattva in ink on hemp *Paintings in Shōsō-in* from the Shōsō-in at Nara, where the scarf floats in lively swirls round the figure. Though possibly only a rough sketch, the freedom FIG. 33 and ease of the brushwork are typical of Japanese painting. The insistence on line is a Far Eastern characteristic; the great figure painters of China here find a reflection among the Japanese. The face has a warm individuality and there is nothing hieratical or stiff in the pose. The gentle swaying of the body, allied with the floating scarf, gives a sense of rhythmic movement. The full compositional powers of the Japanese artist can be seen in the later copy of a design originally painted in A.D. 755 for the doors of the FIG. 34 Kaidan-in. The easy movement, relaxed poses and the command of viewpoint are as accomplished as anything produced by Chinese artists in the T'ang dynasty.

The few relics of Nara painting we have considered are overshad- *Murals in Hōryū-ji* owed by the greatest example of Eastern religious painting, the murals of the Main Hall of the Hōryū-ji — the highest achievement of Mahāyāna Buddhist painting and one peak of development of Far Eastern art. Unfortunately for art history the Main Hall of the PLATE P. 64 temple, itself an architectural monument of great antiquity, was burned through a light left by a careless workman, and as a result the paintings were scorched to little more than black and white outlines. Only some fine colour reproductions, by chance photographed just before the fire by Japan's best art photographer, survive to recall their beauty.

Much controversy has raged regarding their date and even their

identification, but it is now widely held that they were painted about 710 and that the four central panels represent four Buddhas that were particularly popular at the time: Amida, the Buddha of the Western Paradise; Yakushi, the Buddha of Healing; Shākyamuni, the Historical Buddha, and Miroku, the Buddha of the Future. The traditions of wall-painting come from India; the best known early examples have survived at Ajantā and Bāgh. The progress of the faith through Central Asia left many wall-paintings at the oases where the pilgrims rested, and some striking documents have been discovered there. At Tun-huang, where the travellers from India entered China, there are very many paintings but they are all very provincial and of inferior quality compared with the masterpieces of the Hōryū-ji. It is hardly possible that they served as a model for the unknown Japanese artist of the Hōryū-ji.

The figures are outlined in strong red lines and a type of shading is used for emphasis. This is an Indian invention found in a number of Central Asian wall-paintings. The faces, expressions and diaphanous drapery all belong to a common Buddhist vocabulary used throughout Asia. However, the Japanese artists have simplified and spiritualized the compositions, leaving

Fig. 34 – *Late copy of a design of Heavenly Musicians, made for doors in the Kaidan-in. A.D. 755. Cf. p. 75.*

out the crowded riotousness of the Indian models and the disorganization of those of Central Asia. Much is said in Chinese art history of a certain Central Asian painter named Wei-ch'ih I-sêng who is said to have used brush-strokes 'appearing like iron wire bent into shapes'. Nothing of his work has survived, but the tradition has persisted and appears here at the Far Eastern extension of a long line which starts in India and connects the whole artistic world of Buddhism.

The detail shown in the plate on page 62 is a Bodhisattva seated on a lotus flower, from the group depicting the Buddha of Healing. PLATE P. 62 The colours and gentle rhythms of the figure recall some of the best Chinese work at Tun-huang — a combination of vigour and spirituality which is T'ang art at its best. The gay colours and clear detail contribute to this vision of perfect form. The sympathetic tilt of the head and swaying delicacy enchant the worshipper with their vision of bliss. These murals are a fitting climax to the art of the Nara period.

IV. THE EARLY HEIAN PERIOD (794–876)
(KŌNIN, 810–823; JŌGAN, 859–876)

Nagaoka Towards the end of the eighth century the Japanese decided to desert the beautiful city of Nara which they had worked so hard to create and build an entirely new capital at Nagaoka. Nobody knows exactly why they decided to do this. Most historians think that the court wished to escape from the growing power of the Nara clergy, as personified by such overweening intriguers as Dōkyō. If this was indeed their wish it was soon to be frustrated, for the new sects which grew up wherever the court established its capital very soon began to exercise great power. The Japanese also have an old belief dating to pre-Buddhist times that a place is defiled by death. Although in early Japan it was an easy matter to move a palace, since this was a relatively simple type of building, the construction of a whole new city in a different location was a very serious undertaking. This was particularly true in a comparatively poor country such as Japan, where the finances were already strained. We are told that the building of the new city took the labour of 300,000 workers and the revenue from a whole year's taxes.

Heian-kyō Then, after ten years work at Nagaoka, the project was just as suddenly dropped again and a new site chosen at what is the present-day Kyōto; it was named Heian-kyō, or 'The Capital of Peace and Tranquillity'. The reason for this seemingly incomprehensible decision is likewise obscure. However, the building of the Nagaoka site had been accompanied by a number of disasters, culminating in the violent death of the emperor's brother and a series of misfortunes to the imperial family. The spirits, it seemed, were against the project and could only be appeased by leaving the area.

After further hectic labour the emperor was able to occupy his new palace at Kyōto in 793; work continued for another ten years on the main buildings of the rest of the city. Heian-kyō again was fundamentally Chinese in layout, with wide main streets forming a rectangular grid intersected by smaller roads. Kyōtō has, of course, altered a great deal over the centuries and the pace of change has accelerated in recent years, but much still remains to recall the old city. Though the main gates have disappeared, many ancient temples have survived the fires that have always been the enemy of Japanese buildings. Here and there the old waterways can still be seen flowing down from the hill-sides, an illustration of what Cammann called 'the harmonious blend of the aesthetic with the functional that has always characterized Japanese life in general'.

At this time Japan was still under the cultural influence of China but the initial greatness of the T'ang period was already passing. The second half of the T'ang dynasty was marked by increasing unrest throughout the Chinese empire, by the breakdown of the once magnificent administrative system and by insubordination in high places. Nevertheless China was still the Mecca. New Buddhist sects came to Japan which were to change completely the old vision *New sects* of the faith that had given the art of Nara its directness, simplicity and charm. At Nara the old sects remained secure and cut off from the new developments, leaving the field open to later arrivals. Japan was eager for innovation even in religious matters and each importation was eagerly awaited and studied. Men anxious for the security and economic rewards of monastic life could find places in the new monasteries. The court, for its part, hoped that the power of the old sects could be restrained by the vigorous new establishments and therefore backed them. The most important of these sects were the Tendai, introduced in 805 by Dengyō Daishi, 'The Great Teacher Dengyō' as he came to be known, and the Shingon or 'True Word' sect, founded by Kōbō Daishi in 806–7.

The Tendai sect came from China, where it had its headquarters *Tendai* on Mount T'ien-t'ai. Its teaching is fundamentally eclectic, but its core is the doctrine contained in one of the most famous scriptures, the *Lotus Sūtra*. This in essence taught that the absolute is inherent in all phenomena and that all phenomena are manifestations of an unchanging reality. Study of the scriptures, religious practices and

FIG. 35 – *Bronze reliquary in the form of a stūpa (hōtō). Cf. p. 82.*

contemplation were the means to enlightenment. Through study
and correct living a man could attain the Buddha Nature which is
inherent in everybody and everything. The sect insisted on having
its own right of ordination to the priesthood. This was certainly in
order to free itself from the control of the Nara clergy. The court
supported this demand for the same reason: it wished to curb the
Nara clergy's power. The sect had a broad, balanced view of the
means to attain wisdom, which should come through a combination
of all the various media of religious experience. It set up its main
temple on Mount Hiei outside Kyōtō, where it claimed that it
could protect the city from any evil influences coming from the
north-east. The mountain itself became an object of profound
veneration, and it is interesting to see how at this time deeply-
rooted native Japanese animistic beliefs began to find a place in
Japanese forms of Buddhism. The court lent support to the sect,
but in doing so created a source of trouble for itself, since later the
militant clergy on Mount Hiei were to become a great scourge.

Shingon Kōbō Daishi, an urbane artistic man of scholarly bent, returned
from China in 807 with the Shingon or 'True Word' sect, in which
the central place was taken by Dainichi Nyōrai, the Supreme
Eternal Buddha from which all other Buddhas emanate. 'True
Word' refers to the magic formulae which Shingon adherents believe represent the elements of the universe. The sect has its origins
in late Indian Tantric Buddhism, which spread to China, Tibet
and Java, and has affinities with Lamaism. Its followers emphasized
the importance of incantations, spells and magic symbols. Kōbō Daishi
established his temple far from Kyōtō in a dense forest high up in
Wakayama province, which secured it from court intrigue on the
one hand and from rivalry with the Tendai on the other. A visit to
Kōya-san, with its many small temples overshadowed by giant

trees, shrouded in mist through which the sunlight penetrates in thick shafts, is a very moving experience. Kōbō Daishi rapidly gained favour at court, where Shingon beliefs had a considerable appeal. To the Shingon believer consciousness is the same as reality and reality is expressed in the body of Dainichi. The whole universe is an expression of the Buddha Nature. The religion was all-embracing and the many spirits in the conscious world could easily be expressed as different divinities. Above all, for the Shingon follower salvation was quick and easy; these were essential qualities in a sybaritic society. Both Tendai and Shingon were tolerant and accepted other teachings, even the native Shintō, as parts of the more inclusive pattern they claimed to follow. These *mikkyō* — *Mikkyō sects* 'secret' or 'esoteric' sects — offered highly mysterious doctrines which the layman who had hitherto enjoyed a simple creed could not be expected to understand. Imposing religious paraphernalia likewise abounded in complicated Tantric-type images and paintings. In Shingon part of the teachings are open and part secret; public worship often took the form of simply repeating magic formulae. The terrifying aspects of Buddhist divinities played a much larger role than hitherto — especially the Myō-ō, the fearsome kings who protect the faith and punish the evildoer. These mystic teachings must have appealed to a deep strain in the Japanese mentality. The mysterious aspects of Shintō thought struck a responsive chord in ancient native beliefs, which the new sects were happy to incorporate into their teaching. The new faiths certainly reinvigorated Buddhism, which at the end of the Nara period must have seemed effete, secular and even corrupt.

Sir Charles Eliot, summing up the effect of Shingon, says that it 'eliminated numerous dangerous abuses which were growing up, taught noble and profound ideas and gave them worthy expression in art. On the other hand, this profundity and copious use of symbolism was its greatest danger. Its adherents, except those rare spirits who could fathom its deep mysteries, mistook the symbol for the reality and lapsed into polytheism and superstition.'[1]

[1] Sir Charles Eliot, *Japanese Buddhism* (London 1935), p. 239.

Strangely enough, so few original buildings of the period have survived that we know little about any innovations they may have made to architecture. In old cities like Kyōtō the styles of Nara were continued but in the mountain fastnesses, where broad areas of flat land are scarce, the buildings tended to become groups of small structures — which suited the atmosphere of mystery. The sects liked to encourage a *stūpa*-type building, originally intended to house relics of the Buddha — as seen in the bronze reliquary model reproduced here.

FIG. 35

The appeal of Chinese culture was still dominant. Japanese monks travelled through China collecting scriptures and religious objects to bring back to an admiring culture-hungry Japan. Chinese literature was supreme; the T'ang poets were studied so closely that Japanese adepts even imitated to the last detail the settings of the Chinese poems.

SCULPTURE

Opinions are divided on the sculpture of this period. Some see a powerful new artistic spirit reinvigorating a Buddhist art which had grown feeble at the end of the Nara period. Others, who delight in the straightforward uncomplicated religious and artistic formulae of most works of the earlier period, resent the seeming grossness of the new forms, although it must be said that indications of this trend are found in the earlier period. Certainly in its most typical expression the old simplicity gave way to something awe-inspiring, heavy with symbolic meaning and totally divorced from reality. Sculpture was an art of the church following prescribed canons and intended to impress. By now the Japanese craftsmen had firmly chosen wood as their favourite medium and revealed themselves as master carvers. From this time onwards they were to use little else.

Yakushi Nyōrai

PLATE P. 65

The Yakushi Nyōrai in the Gangō-ji, Nara is a typical example of the new approach to Buddhist divinities. It is heavy and massive, totally lacking the sympathy of earlier times. It is carved from a single piece of wood and left unpainted, possibly to reveal the sacred wood. The position is four-square and uncompromising, the face grimly set as if to belie the gesture of 'have no fear' in the hands. Weighty inertia pervades the whole concept. These features must

FIG. 36 – *Detail of a wall-painting from Bezeklik, Central Asia. After F. H. Andrews, Wall-paintings from Ancient Shrines in Central Asia. Cf. p. 84.*

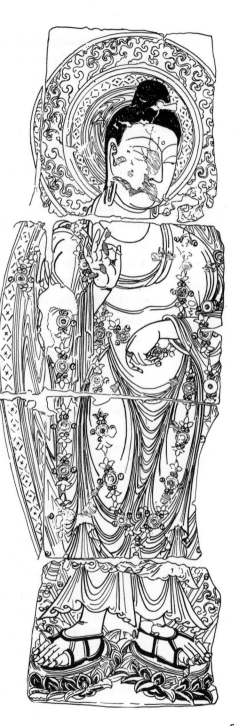

certainly have had a deep religious force, for why else should the Japanese have sacrificed the grace and charm of earlier images?

The craftsmanship is outstanding, especially in the folds of the robe which are in what the Japanese call the *hompa shiki* or 'wave form'. One deep wave-like fold is followed by a shallower wave, leading to another deep one — like waves rippling over the sands, as one writer happily describes them. The control of the relationship between body and drapery is masterly. The whole impression is of heavy grandeur relieved by the rhythm and vitality of the carving. Sherman Lee in a recent book[1] calls their style 'the most awesome style created in the Far East, just as the Byzantine style may well be called the most awesome one created in medieval Europe'; Seiroku Noma sees in it a spiritualism which was needed to reinvigorate sculpture and 'destroy the shell of stifling realism'. It is

[1] Sherman E. Lee, *A History of Far Eastern Art* (London 1964), p. 283.

83

essentially outgoing in its power to awe and subdue, and breathes an air of heavy mystery. These are not gods to whom one could come close.

FIG. 36 The pattern for this type of image comes from the mainland, as far as we know from sites in Central Asia, which are in turn closer to Indian sites. It is as if the Japanese with typical pertinacity were trying to find the source of Chinese Buddhism. The Japanese have made the model in wood heavier and more repellent than the examples in wall-paintings which have survived.

Nyōirin Kannon

PLATE P. 66 The Nyōirin Kannon in the Kanshin-ji, made between about 824 and 827, belongs to the group of secret statues which are only shown on very rare occasions, and then only after lengthy preparation. The care with which it has been kept hidden accounts for its remarkable state of preservation; even the original paint has survived on the flaming nimbus or *mandorla*. Only two of the hands have recently been restored. The figure known in India as Cintāmani-cakra is intended to represent the Goddess of Compassion with the gem and wheel which satisfy all desires. Yashiro describes its effect as a combination of 'sensuous enchantment and spiritual mystery'. Its frank sensuousness may well be due to influences derived from Indian painting which had been incorporated into Chinese sculpture and were found in countless T'ang works. The thick facial features — full lips, ringed neck, languid arms and naturalistic drapery — are all characteristically Chinese T'ang.

Leaving out of account all the aura of secrecy, the effect of the statue wears a little thin, for in a sense the figure is not typical and is highly derivative. It lacks the characteristics which give much of Japanese wood-carving its sensitive quality. It has none of the powerful balefulness of the type previously discussed. The pose is comfortable and relaxed, with an air of worldly superiority. The rather doll-like face is dreamy and preoccupied. The iconographic demands of six arms are skilfully contrived within the easy pose, but one senses that they have slightly hampered the Japanese carver, who is always sensitive to the beauty of the human body, even if he does not study it in the Western anatomical sense. One senses that the Japanese are not fundamentally happy in these physical abnormalities. Nevertheless the figure has an inner warmth which separates it from the grim forbidding world of the Yakushi Nyōrai. It belongs to the realm of painting rather than that of sculpture, perhaps to iconography rather than art!

Just as the sculpture of the early Heian period leaned strongly on iconographical content, so also its painting often tended to be heavily didactic. A favourite form was the *mandara*, which in Sanskrit means 'circle'. In practice this is a complicated and diagrammatic map-like painting which sets out in geometric form the various heavens and their countless deities. Generally 'the Great Illuminator Dainichi' occupies the central position. In some ways this type of painting, which originated in China but does not seem to have found much favour in the country of its origin, suited the Shingon and Tendai sects better than sculpture — precisely because it could express more complicated and involved teachings. It aimed at overwhelming the worshipper with the limitlessness of the suprahuman worlds which awaited him, as well as with the seeming profundity or, at least, complexity of the beliefs held by these sects. Yet at the same time the believer was given reason to hope that a place could be found for him. Such an approach is natural for a form of teaching which leans heavily on mystery. There is an intellectual ponderousness throughout this type of painting which is an integral part of the system. Later historians can appreciate the meticulous draughtsmanship, the fine lines, the thin gold and blue colours, but the works as a whole are inclined to be boring and not so interesting as other forms of painting.

The most vital of the other types of painting introduced in this period express in more detail and with greater emphasis some of the terrifying aspects of the religion which we have already seen in sculpture. We have in mind the paintings of the deity Fudō, one of the Five Great Kings who in turn are emanations of Dainichi. Their function is to protect the Buddhist world and deter the evildoer. The most famous of these is the Aka Fudō or 'Red Fudō' enshrined in the Myōō-in, a temple forming part of the main Shingon complex at Mount Kōya. He sits on naturalistic rocks holding the symbols of his power, a sword and a rope. His face is

PAINTING

Mandara

FIG. 37

Aka Fudō

PLATE P. 67

85

FIG. 37 – *Detail of the Ryōkai Mandara, 'the Mandala of the Two Worlds'. Gold and silver on purple silk. Jingo-ji, Kyōtō. Cf.p. 85.*

PLATE 21 – The Bodhisattva Fūgen (detail). Anonymous. Colour on silk. 12th cent. *160.1 × 73.7 cm*. *National Museum, Tokyo. Cf. p. 104.*

PLATE 22 – Kinkan Shitsugen ('The Buddha Rising from his Golden Coffin', detail). Colour on silk. Anonymous. Late 11th cent. Chōhō-ji Temple, Kyōtō. *161.1 × 228.7 cm. Cf. p. 105.*

PLATE 23 – Muchaku by Unkei and his school. Painted wood. Kōfuku-ji Temple, Nara. *Height 195 cm.*
Cf. p. 122.

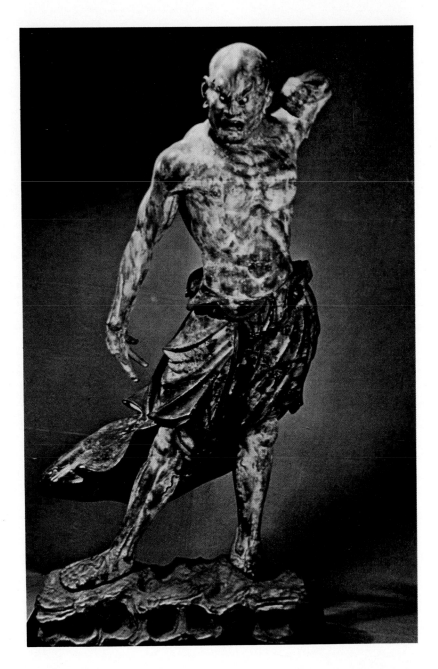

PLATE 24 – Kongō Rikishi by Jōkei. Painted wood. *C.* A.D. 1190–8. Kōfuku-ji Temple, Nara. *Height 162.6 cm. Cf. p. 124.*

PLATE 25 – Uesugi Shigefusa. Wood. Anonymous. Meigetsu-in Temple, Kamakura. *Height 68.6 cm.*
Cf. p. 125.

PLATE 27 – Kōbō Daishi as a boy, (detail). Colour on silk. Anonymous. *45.7 × 38.1 cm. Murayama Collection, Mikage. Cf. p. 128, 130.*

◀ PLATE 26 – Minamoto-no-Yoritomo. Colour on silk. Attributed to Fujiwara Takanobu (1143–1206) Jingo-ji Temple, Kyōtō. *139.8 × 111.8 cm. Cf. p. 126.*

PLATE 28 – Detail from one of the three Shigisan-engi-emaki painted hand-scrolls depicting the history of the Chōgosonshi-ji Temple. Ink and colour on paper. Anonymous. Latter half of 12th cent. *Length of detail 72.4 cm, width 31.8 cm. Cf. p. 132.*

fierce; he has canine teeth and glares angrily out of the picture. The two young acolytes beneath him are Seitaku, who symbolizes the subjugating power, and Kinkara, who stands for the sustaining virtue. The whole composition, which stretches like a bow from top left to bottom left, is dominated by the flaming halo; all are painted in a lurid red colour which adds to the impact. There is a sensuous feeling here which is quite new. Some authorities claim that the free and asymmetrical composition and feeling for depth in this painting indicate a later date than the early Heian to which it is usually attributed. There is no reason why this should be so and the general sense of the work fits early Heian ideals. There were no Chinese parallels for the painting.

The early Heian period introduced new religious and artistic influences which were to have far-reaching effects on later periods. It saw the beginnings of Japanese art proper — more self-conscious, assertive and grandiloquent. But for the full development of this essentially Japanese quality we must consider the development of the arts in the following period.

V. THE LATE HEIAN OR FUJIWARA PERIOD
(895–1185)

Few periods in the history of civilized man can hold more interest than the three centuries covered by the late Heian period. For the first time since the introduction of Chinese civilization over three hundred years earlier Japan began to stand on its own feet politically, socially and culturally.

Breach with China What brought this long honeymoon, this deep enthrallment with Chinese culture to an end? The main factor was that contemporary events in China convinced the Japanese that it would be dangerous for Japan if they did not sever their relations with the mainland. A serious persecution of Buddhism in China in the middle of the ninth century deeply disturbed the Japanese, who were sincerely devoted to the faith and the tolerance it enjoined. Religious tolerance has always distinguished their civilization, and they have never experienced the kind of persecution common in China which brought destruction to so many art treasures. At a very early date Shintō and Buddhism learned to respect each other and live together. Moreover, the administrative system of the great Chinese empire was rapidly disintegrating under the pressures of external attack and internal revolt. The Japanese ruling class feared both these enemies of settled government; the security which their island position afforded had not taught them either how to deal with such problems or how to face them with equanimity.

The political missions from Japan to China, which had been such a feature of earlier centuries, diminished rapidly in number during the ninth century. Scholars and priests continued to travel to China, and the Japanese aristocrats still looked eagerly to that country for luxury articles — art objects, new works of literature, drugs, incense and perfume — which Japan could not produce herself. But by 900 the two countries were politically far apart and visitors from China were not welcomed. Ordinary Japanese were forbidden to travel. The Japanese now began to realize that their society and its problems were different from those of China and required solutions which only they could work out. For example, the overthrow of an imperial house, common in China, could not be tolerated in Japan where the emperor was considered divine, the direct descendant of the gods. Though the Chinese language continued to command respect, a Japanese vernacular language emerged as an accepted vehicle for literature, especially for poetry and romances — of which the famous *Tale of Genji*, by the Lady Murasaki, written between 1008 and 1020, is the outstanding example. She openly criticizes the 'Chinesy' language for its stiffness. That the Japanese could even consider such a breach with China is an indication of the new self-confident atmosphere in this energetic expanding country. *Literature*

This period saw two developments which were to make and mar subsequent centuries. The emperor lost authority, and behind his back strong and ruthless men controlled the destinies of the country; there came into being a feudal society, in which rival factions struggled for power, performing feats of heroism but also bringing considerable misery upon the nation.

The first great family to control the emperor and the country was the Fujiwara, after whom the period is sometimes called. They too claimed descent from the gods; they rose to power gradually from the end of the eighth century by acquiring land and wealth and by forming skilful alliances. The Fujiwara gave their daughters in marriage or concubinage to a succession of emperors, most of whom were relatively weak. They survived all intrigues against them and the numerous offspring from these liaisons further strengthened their hold over the imperial fortunes. Political office was hereditary, and it is understandable that they were not attracted to the more egalitarian Chinese system of entry to the civil service by examination and promotion by merit. They adopted the externals of Confucianism but without the concern for the people which Confucianism encouraged in its public servants. *Fujiwara*

On the whole they were able men, motivated by family pride and a genuine interest in the welfare of the state. Though the literature of the period gives the impression of luxury-loving voluptuaries, politicians like Fujiwara-no-Michinaga must also have been hard-

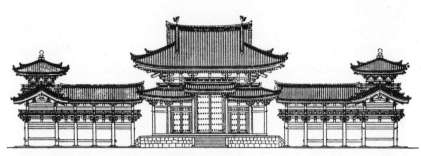

FIG. 38 – *Elevation of the Phoenix Hall of the Byōdō-in at Uji, converted into a temple of Amida Buddha in* A.D. *1052. Cf. p. 102.*

working, serious men, constantly on their guard against rival claimants to power — especially the rapidly increasing number of provincial lords.

The emperors were unable to control the Fujiwara, for their ever-growing lands and incomes were exempt from tax and without money the emperor could not maintain any kind of military or police force to carry out his will. The peaceful centuries of the T'ang dynasty in China had created such a false sense of security that even the national armed forces had deteriorated. The emperor became little more than a cultural dignitary whose powers scarcely went beyond ordering the minutiae of ceremonial. Nevertheless, the system did at least enable the imperial line to survive unbroken. On the other hand, the nepotism and tight control exercised by the Fujiwara made able men disinclined to enter public life; many of the best entered the monasteries, where their talents had great scope. The Fujiwara did not actually have a fighting force of their own but were able to rely upon the support of powerful local lords, between whom they were careful to maintain a balance — albeit an uneasy one. This was their weakness and was to prove their undoing. Behind the refined façade of court life the lords waged a savage battle for power. The nobility began to develop the code of the *samurai* or 'serving man', with its strict code of honour, *bushidō* ('The Way of the Knight'), which governed their behaviour.

It was a system every bit as delicately balanced and as complicated as that of feudal Europe.

The court life which the Fujiwara built up in Kyōtō reached a *Life at court* particular peak of sophistication and refinement from about 966 to 1027. The elegant ladies and gentlemen of the court seem to have drifted like falling maple-leaves through a world whose sensibilities are too fine for us to appreciate. The adjectives that spring to mind are: sentimental, delicate, elegant, refined, artistic, exquisite, melancholy, fatuous. They were luxury-loving, obsessed by the pleasures of seduction and by the more subtle longings of unrequited passion. The trivia of court etiquette and dress absorbed much of their mental energy. They were fascinated by literature and art, which they patronized handsomely. And yet behind all this runs the stream of melancholy which repeatedly comes to the surface in the Japanese character. Japanese civilization developed in an artificial vacuum, in an atmosphere of womanizing and intrigue, isolated from invigorating foreign contacts. It is the world described for us in such clear detail by Lady Murasaki, and which Sir George Sansom has summed up in his eloquent prose as 'a mode of existence dedicated to the acute perception of beauty and the refinement of personal relations to such a point that ideas and feelings could be conveyed by the merest shadow of a hint'.

The church in turn adopted the violent standards of the time and *Religion* became as militant as the provincial lords. The Shingon sect, for the most part, was able to remain in its country fastnesses aloof from the turmoil, but the Tendai, especially in the temples outside Kyōtō, raised armies of mercenaries which would descend at times upon the capital to enforce their claims or indulge in violent sectarian rivalries. Serious Buddhists intensely disliked this attitude, which is so alien to the peaceful tenets of the faith. The court, too, found these militant monks dangerous allies. But these aristocrats comprised only a very small proportion of the population and were completely divorced from the people, who had little sympathy with their life of pleasure and ostentation. The Buddhist church was ripe for a reformation. The people flocked to a new sect, the Jōdō or Pure Land sect, which offered a single salvationist faith based on

worship of the Amida Buddha — the Buddha of the Western Paradise. The means of salvation was simple. One had merely to call upon the name of the Buddha with a simple formula, 'Namu Amida Butsu', for one's sins to be forgiven and to secure entry into paradise. This broadly-based religion, open to all, appealed to the emotions rather than to the intellect — which suited the Japanese character. The attraction of 'pleasure in this world, bliss in the next' was irresistible.

In the Fujiwara period sculpture in a sense returned to the gentler tastes of the Nara period. It discarded the heavy forms and forbidding attitudes of the early Heian — the product of a Buddhism which the court found distasteful. The Fujiwara sybarites had little sympathy with the stern sanctions of Tendai and Shingon — nor did they like the violence which their monks practised. The attractions of the Pure Land sect were more in keeping both with the way of life of the court and the aspirations of the common people.

Another factor was that new temples were springing up throughout the country and the demand for sculpture to furnish them was rapidly increasing. The old method of carving statues from large logs of wood was too slow and cumbersome to meet this demand. Thus the ateliers developed a system of manufacture: a large number of pieces were assembled to form a thin shell, which was then finished off by the master. This method was followed in all the work of this and subsequent periods.

It is interesting to see the emergence of great master sculptors much as in the West. In China sculpture was a humble craft and its greatest exponents are seldom known by name (whereas the painters have been recorded and praised for nearly two thousand years). In Japan the sculptors became men of importance in their own right and patrons eagerly sought their services. The position they gained in society enabled them to impose their own taste on the art of their time much more immediately than if they had been simple artisans carrying out the orders of a temple, following stereo-

◀ FIG. 39 – *Keman in bronze. Chūson-ji Temple, Iwate Prefecture. Length 28.5 cm, width 32.8 cm. Cf. p. 106.*

Fig. 40 – *Kei (gong) in gilt bronze. Zenrin-ji Temple, Kyōtō. Length 19.7 cm. Cf. p. 106.*

typed formulae. This independence in turn reflected on the other arts and crafts, which gained in esteem. No craft was too humble to be turned to artistic use — an attitude which enriched all subsequent Japanese art. The extension of this development enjoined originality in an artist and this too had far-reaching influences on subsequent Japanese art.

The work which summarizes these new trends is the Amida by Jōchō, who established an atelier in Shichijō Street, Kyōtō, and died about 1057. It is housed in the Phoenix Hall of the Byōdō-in at Uji near Kyōtō. The building itself is interesting, for it was originally a private mansion and was later (1052) turned into a temple dedicated to the Amida Buddha. It is inspired by Chinese Sung dynasty architecture on one hand and by the longings of the Pure Land sect on the other; its intention is to reproduce on earth as far as possible the Paradise of the Amida which awaited the faithful in heaven. It is a light and graceful structure which seems to float above the waters of a small lake in a most ethereal way. Jōchō was trained in the Kōfuku-ji Temple workshops at Nara. Thus he was familiar with the simply conceived masterpieces of the old capital and, although he worked in Kyōtō, he showed little sympathy with Tendai and Shingon attitudes.

Amida by Jōchō
PLATE P. 68
FIG. 38

The Jōchō Amida is made of wood which was thinly lacquered. It sits calmly and impassively in the position of meditation, eyes looking straight ahead, in front of a huge nimbus, with an ornate canopy above. Its smooth lines and unadorned simplicity contrast effectively with the complicated carving behind and above. The atmosphere of the statue typifies the changed outlook of the faith — now friendly, welcoming and at rest. The ornate setting of the nimbus, where small figures on lotuses represent souls newly born into paradise, reflects the love of the ornate in court circles. As W. Watson remarks, 'The originality of this formula lies in the new use it makes of the physical proportions for sculptural effect. The power of the image is not confined to the facial expression, but derives from the majestic pose of the whole body.' This figure became the model for countless gilt wood Buddha figures in later centuries. The relative simplicity of the concept made it easy to copy in its more superficial aspects, but constant repetition led to increasing loss of power — a classic example of a great master's design becoming schematized and desiccated.

The real masterpiece of the assembled block technique is the Kichijō-ten in the Jōruri-ji Temple in Kyōtō. This statue is a rich and complicated piece in which the heavy, almost fussy detail — as in the sleeves, jewels, jacket, sash and exquisite hands — is all worked in wood. It was then painted in five colours in what the Japanese call 'rainbow shading', with a red background scattered with gold dust — the whole creating the rich impression befitting a Goddess of Good Fortune. Such a work would have been impossible in the single block technique. The statue recalls the plump beauties of T'ang as seen in the painting of the same subject from the Nara period (see plate on p. 63), but it is here very 'Japanized' to express the delicacy and elegance of late Heian society. The statue may in fact have been made early in the next period, but it is essentially Fujiwara in outlook, in its lively pleasure and keen enjoyment of colour. Its painted shrine makes it look even more resplendent.

The new vision of Amida which Genshin brought and made popular in the Jōdō sect had a far-reaching effect on Buddhist painting. One of the most popular types shows Amida, either alone or accompa-

Kichijō-ten in Jōruri-ji

PLATE P. 69

PLATE P. 63

PAINTING

nied, in scenes which suggest that he is greeting the faithful entering his paradise. Sometimes he is shown as if descending from his heaven through a Japanese-style landscape. The most famous of these

Amida in Daien-in

Amida Paradise paintings is the Amida and the Twenty-five Bodhi-sattvas owned by the Daien-in, a temple of the Shingon head-

PLATE P. 70

quarters on Mount Kōya. In this large triptych the deity is sur-rounded by all his heavenly hosts in an impressive pageant which seems to be floating majestically down to earth. The painting has been attributed to Genshin himself, although this is unlikely. The Bodhisattvas are shown playing musical instruments and dancing in a most seductive manner while the Buddha sits calm and serene, with his two main attendants, Kannon and Seishi, below and on either side. The graduated colouring adds naturalism and warmth to the scene. Everything is spontaneous and relaxed, gay, colourful and rich in detail. This is the kind of vision which the Fujiwara court could appreciate — a paradise peopled with delightful maidens ready to offer them greater bliss than any they knew even in their own world of pleasure. It was equally attractive to the common people whose lot was very different. How far removed is this dream-like vision from the dry schematism of the early Heian mandalas and the grim Fudō!

The trend towards gentle naturalism also influenced the older sects, Tendai and Shingon, which were forced to provide something as attractive as the new Jōdō attitudes. Many images were painted

Fūgen

of the Bodhisattva Fūgen (Sanskrit: Samantabhadra), the com-passionate deity who is the central character of the popular *Lotus*

PLATE P. 87

Sūtra. Here the artist shows him seated on his vehicle, a white elephant, in a calm attitude of prayer, a basically feminine figure with splendid jewellery and pink-toned flesh. The Fujiwara artist has here combined the sensual and spiritual most effectively. The atmosphere is intimate and unpretentious; it makes little appeal to the intellect and achieves a transcendental calm without any of the awesome remoteness of early Heian work.

The Buddha

Perhaps the most impressive of the late Heian religious paintings are those which show the Buddha either in *nirvāna*, the moment when, amidst his sorrowing disciples, his earthly life ended, or the miracle in which he emerges in splendour from his golden coffin to PLATE P. 88 preach the law. This is a famous example and one which seems to be Japanese in origin, for nothing comparable has survived from. China. The artist shows great skill in handling a large and animated scene. All the various Buddhas, Bodhisattvas and holy persons, including his mother, crowd around in surprise to await his sermon. His body shines with a golden light which seems to illuminate the whole scene. The various characters are portrayed with marked individuality. The atmosphere of drama is skilfully exploited but not overplayed. Here in a religious work are shown some of the characteristics of Japanese painting — the portraiture, drama and animation — which distinguish it later.

FIG. 41 – *Design of cranes and plants on back of a bronze mirror. Diameter 24.5 cm. Cf. p. 106.*

Kiri-kane   All three paintings use a characteristic Japanese system of decoration in which gold leaf cut into very fine threads is applied for lines. This *kiri-kane* technique gives many paintings of the period an unusually rich appearance; it was a considerable technical as well as artistic achievement to make such fine designs by this difficult method.

METALWORK   While the ceramics of the Heian period lagged far behind those of China, the metal-workers produced much which in quality and design began to surpass the products of China and to reflect characteristics of native Japanese art. We have excellent examples of metalwork from the Nara period, and the Heian products continued the tradition. The general sense of richness and ebullience is inherited from T'ang China but to this the Japanese added a warmth and pictorial quality that is their own. The *keman* in Figure 39 is a

FIG. 39   metal substitute for what was originally a wreath of flowers used in Buddhist temples; the bow incorporated into the design reveals its origin. The floral background is of peony-like flowers which are in fact imaginary and of Indian origin. The two figures with birds' bodies and youthful faces are intended to represent auspicious birds which, according to Indian lore, live in the mountains and sing beautifully. Even in such a craft work the Japanese manage to synthesize their aesthetic and technical gifts and to show a lively interest in and enjoyment of the colourful world about them.

FIG. 40   The *kei* in Figure 40 is a type of gong that hangs on a rack before a Buddhist image and is struck from time to time by the priests during the recitation of *sūtras*. The lotus arabesques around a central lotus flower, at the point where the gong is struck, and the crisp all-over design have sufficient variety to give it a lively rhythm. The design is repeated on both sides; the gilding is rare for the type. In such designs the Japanese seem to be well up to Chinese standards; if anything they anticipate what the Chinese were to do with red lacquer centuries later.

The two objects above are Japanese but inspired by the Chinese approach to design. Illustrative of the new Japanese approach is

FIG. 41   the back of a metal mirror in Figure 41. Here two herons, one flying with a branch in its beak and the other standing on one foot, are placed asymmetrically in an aquatic landscape. The plants are bending under a strong wind so that they follow the curve of the mirror's rim. The tendency to substitute for the Chinese all-over repetitive pattern a single design in which a naturalistic motif is combined with stylized plants became increasingly strong in subsequent centuries. It gives the Japanese decorative sense a unique quality which distinguishes pottery, textile and lacquer as much as metalwork. The ebullience with which the design spills over the rim, the variety of leaves and their cunning arrangement are essentially Japanese, and find expression in an eighteenth-century plate as clearly as in this early mirror.

From about 1068 the power of the Fujiwara family declined. The female line, which had dominated many emperors, became weak or even barren and dissensions arose even within the Fujiwara ranks. New men relying on their own talents came to the fore and the provincial lords gained increasing influence. The central government was approaching bankruptcy from its lavish expenditure and the dwindling tax returns could not replenish the treasury. The stage was set for the assumption of power by new and more vigorous leaders.

VI. THE KAMAKURA PERIOD (1185–1392)

Decline of imperial house As the power of the Fujiwara family declined, the emperor found himself forced to depend to an increasing degree on the strength of the various local lords throughout Japan for his ultimate authority. This eventually placed him completely in their hands. Although hitherto he had been relatively safe as long as none of them gained any predominant degree of power, it was only a question of time before he would be unable to maintain the balance and one among them would take over real power in the land. The weakness of the emperor stimulated this tendency, for it encouraged the provincial chieftains to disobey central directives whenever, as was so often bound to happen, their own interests were at stake. Revolts were frequent and much blood was shed in putting them down. The rivalry between the various lords finally reduced itself to a battle for power between two noble clans — the Taira and the Minamoto, both of which were closely connected by blood with the imperial house and whose economic interests often coincided. The transfer of power to the landed aristocracy was the main change in political life from about A.D. 900 onwards and during the Kamakura century the process was speeded up. The subsequent history of Japan can be written around the ensuing struggles and the effort to achieve political stability.

Samurai Along with these inter-clan rivalries went the perfection of the organization of a military caste, known generally as the *samurai*. This had arisen in the first place from the need of the small farmers in outlying areas, particularly in the east, to protect themselves on one hand from the attacks of unruly tribes, outcasts, rebels and other lords and on the other from the rapacity of the central authorities. In return for a fee, they put themselves under the protection of a large landowner who for his part was obliged to raise an army to meet his side of the bargain. The private armies which thus grew up were a common feature of the local and metropolitan scene and, until the victory of the Minamoto, a constant source of concern. The serving men of the lords, the samurai, swore absolute personal loyalty to their chieftains and were closely allied to them by economic and marital ties. Their code of honour, *bushidō* ('the Way of the Knight'), has its romantic and attractive side, much emphasized in literature. It resulted in deeds of great heroism, but to the Westerner the exploits of these heroes, so often doomed to eventual disaster, seem coloured by excessive cruelty, treachery, betrayal and fratricide. However, to understand the psyche of the Japanese even in recent times, one must appreciate the complexities of the *samurai* code.

Once successful, the Minamoto established their headquarters at Kamakura, some three hundred miles north-east of Kyōtō. This was the first time that the capital of the country had been outside the Kyōtō – Nara area. In making this change the stern warriors were doubtless activated by a desire to remove their fighting men from the enervating influence of court life — much though many of them may have secretly envied it. Yoritomo, as commander-in-chief, forbade his vassals to enter the court. Kyōtō remained a showplace, a leisured city of temples and palaces, made colourful by empty ceremonies but for a time completely deprived of power. It is significant that the imperial line survived and continues to exist today.

Minamoto

Minamoto-no-Yoritomo, the victor in the struggle for power, was fully conscious of the need for change, although at first he probably did not fully appreciate the responsibilities which his position conferred upon him. He probably thought of himself as *primus inter pares*. He was prepared to use the emperor as a means to an and — that of controlling men as violent and ruthless as himself and of protecting his own interests. He relied completely upon his vassals and was determined, by just recognition of their services, to keep them content and, by rigid discipline, to secure their obedience.

In this atmosphere of political and social change many good men of humble origin who had been unable to find employment in the privilege-ridden world of Kyōtō flocked to join Yoritomo in Kamakura, where their administrative talents were welcomed and their manners helped to leaven the rough military camp atmosphere. As always in Eastern countries, the rulers of Kamakura soon found it expedient to clothe their power in a mantle of respectability and learning. The Kamakura shōguns were soon to learn that the blandishments of court life were more powerful than the imperial armies.

The Kamakura military were on the whole just if somewhat harsh rulers, especially in the division of land which was their fundamental interest. But what started as a military dictatorship soon took on the familiar pattern of the Japanese division of power. Oddly enough the Hōjō family, which followed the Minamoto and took over the real power, were descended from the Taira whom Yoritomo had defeated. It is worth quoting Sansom on the situation in the thirteenth century, which presented 'the astonishing spectacle of a state at the head of which stood a titular emperor whose vestigial functions had been usurped by an abdicated emperor, and whose real power was normally delegated to an hereditary military dictator but was actually wielded by an hereditary adviser of that dictator.' Only the Japanese could make such a system work.

Hōjō

SCULPTURE   The Kamakura proved to be the last great age of Japanese sculpture, reaching a brilliant peak from about 1250 to 1400. Schools and ateliers grew up in Kyōtō and Nara and the demand for sculpture was tremendous. The most famous of these ateliers were the *In* and *En* schools in Kyōtō and the Kei school in Nara, to which belonged the best-known artists Unkei, Kaikei and Jōkei — the names which dominated the age. With the transfer of power into the hands of power politicians, the atmosphere in the arts changed radically. Gone was the gentle seductive charm of the late Fujiwara, with its visions of sweetness and ideal beauty. Its place was taken by the sturdy naturalism which distinguishes Kamakura taste. Figures of gods and priests now became faithful reproductions of worldly beings carved completely in the round, and clothed with drapery so convincingly represented as to invite touch. Even the eyes are crystal insets, glistening with startling reality in the temple lights. Separately carved jewels and swords give added naturalism to the figures. The effect is one of directness which, allied to the Japanese gift for

PLATE 29 – Detail from one of the three Heiji-monogatari-emaki painted hand-scrolls. Ink and colour on paper. Anonymous. Mid-13th cent. *Width 41.9 cm. National Museum, Tokyo. Cf. p. 130, 133.*

PLATE 30 – Detail from the Jigoku Sōshi or 'Hell Scroll'. Painted hand-scroll. Ink and colour on paper. Anonymous. C. 1180. *Hara Collection, Japan. Cf. p. 143.*

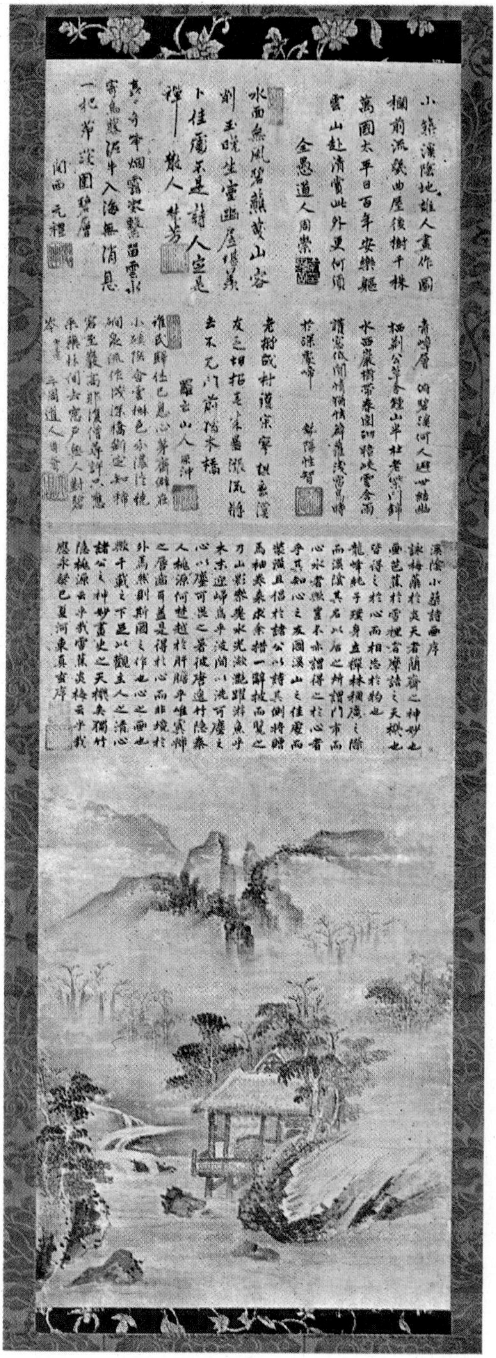

PLATE 31 – Detail from 'Hermitage by a Mountain Brook', attributed to Minchō (Chō Densu, 1352–1431). Ink on paper. Konchi-in Temple, Kyōtō. *100.7 × 33.6 cm. Cf. p. 153*

PLATE 33 – 'Catfish and Gourd' by Josetsu (active *c.* 1405–30). Ink and soft colours on paper. Taizō-in, Kyōtō. *Height 83.2 cm. Cf. p. 155.*

◄ PLATE 32 – 'Kanzan' by Kaō (14th cent.). Ink on paper. *97.9 × 34.3 cm. Nagao Museum, Kanagawa. Cf. p. 154.*

PLATE 35 – 'Winter Landscape' by Sesshū (1420–1506). Ink and soft colours on paper. *45.7* × *27.9 cm.* *National Museum, Tokyo. Cf. p. 157.*

PLATE 34 – 'Studio of the Three Worthies' by Shūbun. Ink and soft colours on paper. 1418. *Seikadō Foundation, Tokyo. Cf. p. 156.*

PLATE 36 – Ama-no-Hashidate by Sesshū (1420–1506). Ink and slight colour on paper. *88.9 × 178.2 cm. National Commission for the Protection of Cultural Properties, Tokyo. Cf. p. 158.*

FIG. 42 – *Shari-den (Hall for Sacred Ashes) in Engaku-ji Temple, Kamakura. Cf. p. 121.*

the representation of surface textures and faithful portraiture, is often disturbing in its impact.

It is interesting to question what produced this new approach. Japanese historians credit it to the civil wars of 1180, which resulted in damage to or destruction of many of the masterpieces of Nara. When peace and order returned, the new masters ordered the workshops to repair and replace the losses. This brought the craftsmen into the closest possible contact with the great masterpieces of the Nara period. Certainly the new interest in the literature and art of the past played a great part in the flowering of Japanese art. Not only were arms and legs repaired and replaced but facsimiles of lost works were made. The art of Nara which circumstances thus forced the craftsmen to study had a simplicity of approach which appealed to the Kamakura. But whereas the Nara sculptors had striven to represent an inner spirituality, the directness of

New interest in Nara art

Kamakura influence, impressive though it may often be, is fundamentally on the surface. This is not to deny the deep appeal which some of the portrait sculptures have, but the approach is sophisticated, even sometimes in its rejection of sophistication. Some critics disagree with this opinion but Kamakura art is essentially outgoing, dynamic rather than contemplative, humanly martial rather than spiritually so.

Shinran and Nichiren sects

This was partly due to the fact that the new Buddhist sects such as the Shin sect founded by Shinran (1173–1262) and the Nichiren sect founded by Nichiren (1222–82) addressed themselves increasingly to the common man and even for the first time to women. These classes demanded an uncomplicated approach so unlike that of the Fujiwara theologians. In an age when great personalities strode the political stage we find the religion of the times celebrating its own heroes.

Contacts with China resumed

It is, on the other hand, possible to overestimate the influence of Nara. For Japan was emerging from its period of isolation from China, its source of spiritual nourishment. At the end of the Fujiwara period Japanese priests were able to re-establish contact and a new era of exchange of religious knowledge and art began. We learn that the priest Chōgen, who restored the Tōdai-ji Temple, visited China no less than three times, which enabled him to transmit the brilliant artistic ideals of the Sung dynasty (A.D. 960–1279). The Great Buddha of the Tōdai-ji was restored with the aid of Chinese workers, and Sung architecture became the fashion — especially in Kamakura, where examples of Sung style building are still to be found. The graceful proportions and the elegance of the structures recall in miniature the great days of Sung China, just as Nara brings T'ang China to life. The inspiration of Sung sculpture was equally evident, as recent discoveries in China emphasize (see below).

ARCHITECTURE

Architecture during the Kamakura period is a most complex subject. Soper, in the best account hitherto given,[1] attributes to it 'an

[1] A. Soper in R. T. Paine and A. Soper, *The Art and Architecture of Japan* (London 1955), p. 233.

almost anarchic variety'. The restorations which the civil wars made necessary compelled the architects to turn back to Nara period styles; this was also the case in sculpture, as we shall see. In addition exotic Chinese styles, mainly from the south of China, came in to mingle with native developments of earlier styles. A so-called 'Indian style', though heavy and ornate, seems to have had no relationship with India and it too probably originated in the South China coast areas. The influence of the newly popular Zen sect (of which we shall say more in the next chapter) on the Chinese styles was strong, for Japanese Zen priests went to China to study temples they wished to reproduce in Japan. In the Zen temples the halls tended to be large and bare to house the assembled clergy — their symmetry being broken only by a lecture platform with stairs going up to it and a large throne for the abbot. Surrounding this hall there was generally a plain corridor.

SCULPTURE

Broadly speaking, Kamakura sculpture shows two main trends. On the one hand the grace and elegance of Sung styles (though on a much lower scale) was something which a population brought up on Fujiwara taste would readily appreciate. On the other hand the more austere tendencies of the early Kamakura warriors were more in sympathy with Zen architectural ideals. Yoritomo, like imperial patrons before him, provided finance for such major rebuilding projects as that of the Tōdai-ji Temple and priests like Chōgen were given facilities to study and work in China before returning to their labours in Japan.

FIG. 42

The Shari-den (Hall for Sacred Ashes) in the Engaku-ji Temple at Kamakura is the only surviving building of the original Five Great Zen Temples of Kamakura. Paradoxically, although it is a Zen temple, it is in the Chinese style brought over by a Chinese priest. Characteristic is the compact bracketing system which fills all the area under the eaves. However, what might have tended to create an over-heavy appearance was softened by making parts of the brackets more slender, with graceful curves. Unfortunately the top-heavy thatched roof is a later restoration replacing the original, which had a much lower pitch more in keeping with the general proportions.

FIG. 43 – *Main Hall of Saimyō-ji Temple, Kyōtō. Cf. below.*

FIG. 43 The Main Hall of the Saimyō-ji Temple near Kyōtō has a mixture of various elements but is nearer to the Kamakura spirit with its square simple plan, low elevation and porch at the front.

Zen, although popular, was not a broadly based religion. Other new Buddhist sects catered for the common man and in doing so demanded symbols which were easy to understand. One result was that portrait artists came into their own.

Muchaku and Seshin The perfection of Japanese classicist portraiture is seen in the two *in Kōfuku-ji* larger than life-size figures of Asanga and Vasubandhu in the PLATE P. 89 Kōfuku-ji Temple at Nara. These two Indian priests, known in Japanese as Muchaku and Seshin, are said to have lived one thousand years after the *nirvāna* of the Buddha and to have formulated the teachings of the Hossō sect to which the Kōfuku-ji belongs. The statues were begun in 1208 under the supervision of Unkei and completed with the help of his six sons and two pupils.

The thick-set bodies of the two priests are carved completely in the round with every possible attention to naturalism. The heavy folds of the robes swing across the bodies in heavy rhythms and fall with natural ease in long sleeves. The upright stance and heavy features are the essence of pugnacious faith. The asymmetrical pose adds to the impression of restrained power. In the intense face with its deep-set eyes, strong lips and large nose nothing is idealized. The bones and muscles, the good and bad features are subjected to a new critical faculty.

It is interesting to compare these portraits with the idealized portraits of the Nara period. There the artist concentrated on the PLATE P. 45 emotive appeal of the inner spirit. The image is already a god or a demi-god, a saint as we would call him in Christian art. The Kamakura priests are men among men, with their human qualities magnified to heroic proportions. The fighting qualities of the *samurai* are reflected in their austere powerful bodies — they are in fact men who would respond to a call to arms as willingly as any warrior. Similarly, they are the kind of images to which a warrior would respond. The distractions of a complicated iconography have disappeared. Their faces reflect the struggles of the faith against human problems. The simplicity, the calm assumptions of Nara times could not be reproduced in an age like the Kamakura, which had seen such bitterness and violence. Above all the simple ecstasy of the Nara faith has disappeared.

Once again, although one is tempted to see in these superb portraits a purely Japanese development, one must turn to China for the prototype. Sung period (A.D. 960–1279) sculpture shows a similar concentration on surface textures and true-to-life physical features, on portraiture rather than divinity. In the cave-temple site of Mai-chi-shan, only recently re-discovered, are figures of FIG. 44 priests which could be the prototypes for the Kōfuku-ji figures. Through their skill with the chisel the Japanese have refined the Chinese prototypes, as was so often the case, and raised them to a level surpassing that of the original. It is from such adaptations and developments that Japanese culture has acquired its reputation as derivative — often quite unjustifiably.

It would be unfair to attribute the violence seen in Kamakura FIG. 45 imagery entirely to the new social climate. The more violent aspects of Buddhist iconography are familiar from the *lokapāla* or Guardians of the Faith in Nara times and from the terrifying Fudō of early Heian. However, they did appeal to a violent streak in the Japanese temperament, to that element of extremism which has from time to

FIG. 44 – *Lohan or priest in Cave 90, Mai-chi-shan, North China. Clay. Heavily restored in the Sung period. Cf. p. 123.*

time surprised those who do not appreciate its origins. Change in Japan has always been sudden and often accompanied by violence, as with the introduction of Chinese or Western culture. At the same time discipline is always strong so that, when it is temporarily removed, the pendulum takes a full and rapid swing towards complete lack of restraint. It is easy to understand that, in a period like the Kamakura, war-like deities strike a sympathetic note and their attributes are readily understood.

Kongō Rikishi
PLATE P. 90

Thus the Kongō Rikishi in the plate on p. 90 is one of a long line of Guardians of the Faith (Vajrapāni). It was probably made by Jōkei during the period A.D. 1190–8. The plastic qualities of this statue dominate: knotted muscles stand out on the bare torso; veins and sinews seem to show through the stretched skin; the moment of striking is held in suspended motion. The movement of the robe, as if caught in a sudden wind, or like that of a bow drawn taut, emphasizes the composition. The only softening feature is the play of the decoration on the robe. The closely-set crystal eyes pierce the spectator; the wide-open mouth symbolizes the power that emanates

from the image. In the violent exaggerated action of these Kamakura 'Vajra-bearers' every plane is conceived in terms of restlessness
and movement; the eye is never allowed to rest. Yet the balance,
so easily destroyed in less capable hands, is here perfectly maintained. The sculptor has risen to the challenge of complex detail
which tested his virtuosity. It is an exaggeration which was to lead
later sculptors into danger, but here it is restrained. Once again
the model for this type comes from China and Mai-chi-shan pro- FIG. 45
vides one clue.

During the Kamakura period a completely new type of sculpture
entered the artists' repertoire. It is quite different from the work of
the Buddhist schools, although to some extent it was foreshadowed
by the Muchaku and Seshin of the early thirteenth century and
even by a few earlier works. Just as priests found themselves celebrated in portraits so, in an age when personalities counted for
much, some outstanding warriors and statesmen were not averse to
having their likenesses carved. The ostensible purpose of such
commemorative works was perhaps to recognize their services on
behalf of a particular temple. Such men were, after all, relatively
insecure *vis-à-vis* those whose power they were usurping, and what
better means could they have of asserting their position than a
portrait? The finest example of these secular statues is that of
Uesugi Shigefusa, housed in the Meigetsu-in, a small temple de- PLATE P. 91
pendent on the larger Zenkō-ji near Kamakura. *Uesugi Shigefusa*

Little is known about the man himself but he seems to have played
a relatively small part in the history of the age. He settled at Kamakura in 1252 and the statue was probably made some years later,
to be housed in the temple which he patronized. The assembled
block technique made it possible to construct a figure of such strange
shape — almost geometrical in its two triangular legs and square-cut
body. The whole figure is pyramidal, leading to the round face
carved from a single block of wood. This gives it a characteristic
stability and balance. The sculptor was obviously fascinated by the
formal court robes, which were originally painted on a lacquer-
impregnated cloth covering the joints. The decoration of these has
now disappeared, leaving only the white undercoat. The gentle

symmetrical billows of the trousers, the stiff flat front, the folds dropping from the shoulders and the wide sleeves have their particular rhythmic beauty.

The face of Shigefusa is in no way an idealized portrait. It has the strength but none of the cold cruelty of Yoritomo, which we shall discuss next. The stiff dress, which is graceful but impersonal, sets off the highly personalized face. The slight forward bend of the head adds a contemplative air. Full lips reveal a very worldly sensuality and only the eyes have a strong oriental cast. The soft hands are those of the courtier rather than the warrior. The whole work is very organically composed, and the light and shade create a sense of solidity and change. Above all, one senses an inner relaxation within the most formal and stiff exterior. This helps to dissolve the artificiality and makes credible what is otherwise an exaggerated concept. In such a work two characteristics of Japanese art, the dramatic and the lyrical, are perfectly harmonized. The genius of the craftsman lies in his depiction of pride without arrogance, power without cruelty and formality without stiffness.

Minamoto-no-Yoritomo

From the sculpture of Shigefusa it is only a step to the portrait painting of Minamoto-no-Yoritomo. This is one of four portraits of great politicians kept in the Jingo-ji Temple, Kyōtō, and attributed on good authority to Fujiwara Takanobu, the painter and poet (1143–1206). Minamoto-no-Yoritomo was the main enemy of the Taira clan. In exile in the eastern provinces he built up his forces, winning important warrior families to his side until he was ready to strike down his enemies. By the time of his death in 1199 he had founded the Kamakura régime and created a ruling class out of a warrior caste. A subtle intriguer, he was also a decisive leader who ruthlessly disposed of all rivals, including even his popular younger brother Yoshitsune, of whom he was jealous. The struggle between the two brothers is one of the sagas of Japanese history, endlessly sung in romance and drama.

PLATE P. 92

Although sometimes brutal, on the whole he dealt justly with his

FIG. 45 – *Guardian. Clay. 6th century. Heavily restored and remodelled in Sung period.* ▶
Left of the gallery outside Cave 4, Mai-chi-shan, North China. Cf. p. 123.

retainers. He was suspicious, but in a period when suspicion was probably justified. Above all he was a skilful politician whose every action was directed towards fulfilling his overall plan to win control of the country. The Japanese derive some amusement by pointing to one of his few human characteristics – a fear of his wife! His portrait shows what one would expect, a man of steely purpose, unpleasant perhaps but serious and long-sighted, an able administrator with whom nobody trifled. He was cold and often may have seemed inhuman, but he was a man of revolutionary zeal who knew whither he was taking the country and was supremely confident in his ability to do so. Having achieved power, he was ready to act with generosity and employ men who had something to contribute. He was cautious and at all times statesmanlike. The hard and cunning side of his nature is obvious in this uncompromising portrait; one can perhaps read into it also a streak of treachery. It is a grim and humourless face, but typical of the leaders of Japan's military caste; it is a face one occasionally meets in the higher echelons of modern Japanese business life. As a composition the outlines are stark and the colours sombre. The ceremonial robe and cap create a solemn impression, the robe leading the spectator's eye with almost geometric precision to the pale set face. Should this prove insufficient, the staff of office underlines the direction of interest. From beneath the robes emerges the hilt of a sword, the real symbol of his power, the final authority in a violent ambitious age.

Chinsō portraits The Japanese artists' gifts for portraiture were not restricted to warriors. Many priests were celebrated in a type of portrait painting known known as *chinsō*, in which these patriarchs of imposing mien are generally shown seated on thrones. This is a type of Zen-inspired likeness which probably originated on the mainland in T'ang times, although few originals from that time have survived. More have come down to us from Kamakura Japan. The fondness for such portraits led the Japanese to depict children, both in sculpture and in painting. Imaginary likenesses of the young prince Shōtoku were popular. However, the plate on p. 93 shows Kōbō Daishi, the great scholar-priest who introduced the Shingon sect to Japan

Kōbō Daishi
PLATE P. 93

(see page 80), as a child of five or six. Tradition tells how he had a dream in which he saw himself seated on an eight-petalled lotus discussing the principles of Buddhism with various deities. His beautiful costume, which is decorated with flowers in silver against a white background, acts as a perfect foil to the child-like serious face and the hands locked in prayer. As Paine has said, 'The charm of realistically presented childhood is united to the easily understood symbols of the halo and the lotus throne to make a very moving and sincere Buddhist picture... the appeal is a twofold one of everyday human emotions joined with the sentiments of hero worship.'[1] The love of children and what would now be called the cult of personality are two strong features of the Japanese mentality, but it is rare to find them thus united.

It is when we come to the scroll-painting of the Kamakura period that Japanese art comes into its own, as most historians agree. This is mainly due to the art form known as *e-makimono* or 'painted scrolls'. These are long hand-scrolls, usually not more than about 12 to 14 inches wide and anything up to 40 feet long. They are unrolled from right to left and viewed in sections contained in a comfortable arm's width. Although in many respects unique to Japan, their degree of independence from Chinese examples is not complete. The scroll form is, of course, Chinese in origin but there it was used mainly for landscape themes illustrating long journeys through mountainous countryside. The Chinese seem to have shown comparatively little interest in genre subjects, whereas these have always absorbed the Japanese. So, too, the typical Japanese scroll colouring with its flat areas of colour, dominated by blue, green and gold but used to express a peculiarly soft Japanese landscape, stems ultimately from T'ang China. However, the use the Japanese made of these two basic techniques in their *e-makimono* produced a unique art form of the greatest interest. The scrolls thus provide a most faithful mirror of the life and times of the Japanese in these early centuries. The early Japanese *e-makimono* painters used a number of different techniques. Some are in black and white only,

SCROLL-PAINTING

E-makimono

[1] Paine and Soper, *op. cit.*, p. 64.

FIG. 46

PLATES PP. 93, 111

some are in full colour, and combinations of the two are also found. Sometimes, in the most ingenious style, the picture forms a continuous story; elsewhere the pictures are split up by the insertion of textual passages which explain the various paintings.

The skill and interest of many of these scrolls lie in the way in which they tell a story in unbroken sequence by the clever use of shifting perspectives and methods of carrying the spectator from one scene to the next. The action thus seems effortlessly continuous; in many scrolls the painters skilfully change the tempo to suit the mood of the painting or the story portrayed. Within the general scroll form the artists developed a remarkable freedom to include or exclude irrelevant detail from their compositions, emphasizing those aspects

FIG. 46 – *Detail of the Chōjū-giga or 'Animal Scrolls'. Ink on paper. Attributed to Toba Sōjō (1052–1140), but probably late 12th cent. Kōzan-ji Temple, Kyōtō. Height 30.5 cm. Cf. pp. 130, 133.*

most pertinent to the story. They could reveal the scene from any angle they wanted, often removing roofs if necessary to show what was going on inside a house; backgrounds could change at will and the essentials of the action were always maintained. No demands of fixed perspective disturbed them and the story always moves on with speed and continuity. The artists always skilfully create and maintain a sense of illusion and drama — often by means of carefully placed areas of cloud or groups of trees which effect the transition in time and place.

As mentioned above, there is nothing particularly original to the Japanese in the basic form of this type of scroll-painting. Early Chinese examples illustrating Buddhist themes are found as early as *c.* A.D. 500 at Tun-huang and the Japanese Tamamushi shrine is another early example of continuous narrative in vertical rather than horizontal form. Their interest derives from the high degree to which the Japanese developed them. They reveal the Japanese taste for drama and a sustained emotion that is unrivalled in Far Eastern art. The drama may be humorous or tragic, secular or religious, mundane or spiritual — but it is always essentially human. In their art the Japanese are more often concerned than the Chinese with man and his problems: his pettiness, his triumphs, the whole gamut of his emotions. The Chinese show more interest in grand transcendental themes, such as overpowering landscapes. Man is almost always subordinate; even their sages, whom we see contemplating in the solitude of nature, are beings whose emotions are distant from our understanding. The native Japanese interest is linked to human conditions and fate. Thus much of Japanese art is in an intimate key which an uninstructed Westerner can immediately understand. The setting may be strange but the emotions are universal. Above all, the *e-makimono* show how the Japanese can take a basic idea from the Chinese and re-work it into a completely new art form. We shall see another brilliant example of this ability in the colour-prints of the Tokugawa period.

One of the most typical scrolls is the *Shigisan-engi*, or History of Mount Shigi, which tells the story of various incidents in the life of the famous priest Myōren. One scroll tells how he used to secure

PLATE P. 42

Shigisan-engi

FIG. 47 – *Detail from the painted hand-scroll 'The Mongol Invasion'. Ink on paper. Anonymous. Imperial Household Collection, Tokyo. Cf. p. 134.*

alms from a rich man by making his alms bowl fly to the home of his patron, who filled it. One day the man ignored the golden bowl. To punish him Myōren made it rise and carry off the man's storehouse, with all its rice sacks, to the priest's mountain retreat. One section often illustrated shows the consternation of his household when they see his storehouse disappearing through the air. The PLATE P. 94 section illustrated in the plate on page 94 is less familiar. The rich man had gone to entreat with the priest, who kept the storehouse for his own purposes and flew the sacks of grain back to his home.

Here we see the surprise and delight of the women of the household — all the menfolk being away on the mountain — when the sacks came flying back. The consternation felt at their disappearance has gone, as has also the sense of urgency. But all the emotions, the drama and tension, the humour of the genre are well illustrated. Other scrolls in the *Shigisan-engi* series recount the histories of the founding of various sects and temples. It is unfortunate that reproduction in books makes it impossible to convey the sense of continuity of the long scrolls.

The 'Animal Scrolls', a small part of which is reproduced in Figure 46, belong to another and somewhat surprising type. They are attributed to a certain priest named Toba Sōjō, although he is unlikely to have been the author. The peculiar and unexplained feature of these scrolls is that they are sometimes quite sacrilegious. Many of them are just amusing animal scenes, but the section illustrated shows a frog masquerading as a Buddha and a priest in the form of a monkey worshipping him. They are in black and white only and the draughtsmanship is splendidly accurate. Were the irreligious scenes the product of a priest-painter with an acute sense of humour mocking the attitudes of some of the less worthy priests of the time?

In a heroic age such as the Kamakura one would expect the artist with an eye for the contemporary scene to seize on some of the most exciting moments of the period. The plate on page 111 is a scene from the *Heiji Monogatari*, a most exciting tale of high and ruthless politics in the Heiji War between two court nobles for supremacy. The scene represented here is not the famous burning of the Sanjō Palace, in the Museum of Fine Arts, Boston, with its wonderful scenes of fire and panic but a slightly quieter, though no less dramatic moment in which Nijō Tennō, the seventeen-year-old emperor, escapes from the palace dressed as a lady-in-waiting and seeks refuge with Taira Kiyomori. This was a key episode in the struggle of the Minamoto against the Taira which led to the foundation of the shōgunate at Kamakura. Under the brilliant Kiyomori the Taira were at first successful in the struggle but later the Minamoto gained supremacy. The object of the young emperor's escape

'Animal Scrolls'
FIG. 46

PLATE P. 111
Heiji Monogatari

133

was to free himself from the control of the former emperor, Gō-Shirakawa, who, although officially in retirement, was still in fact exercising real power.

A moment of national heroism is shown in Figure 47 from *The Story of the Mongol Invasion*. To understand the background to this, a very early example of eye-witness war reporting in pictorial form, one must recount the most outstanding event of the Kamakura period. In 1263 Khubilai, khan of the Mongols, made himself emperor of China and founded the Yüan dynasty. The merciless Mongol fighters swept through Asia into Europe, pillaging and destroying everybody and everything which offered any resistance. In 1268 the Mongol emperor, secure in China and convinced of the irresistible strength of his armies, made his first approach to Japan and suggested that relations should be established. This was tantamount to commanding the Japanese to surrender under pain of dire penalties. The Kamakura warriors, although fully conscious of the significance of their actions, refused to comply. This was the equivalent of a declaration of war. The Mongols spent a year preparing a fleet of about 450 ships, 15,000 Mongol troops and an equal number of Korean auxiliaries. They confidently landed on the west coast of the southern island where they were met with determination and courage by the local chieftains and their retainers. After a day of heavy fighting honours were even and the Mongols returned to their fleet. However, in the night a heavy storm scattered and destroyed their ships. The losses are said to have been 13,000 men and an unaccustomed blow to Mongol prestige.

By 1280 Khubilai had mustered another force of no less than 150,000 men for a second attempt on the stubborn Japanese. The invasion of 1281 led to fifty days of heavy fighting and again a storm drove the invaders from the Japanese coast. This time they lost four-fifths of their forces and, although the threat of invasion lasted for another twenty years, the Japanese were left alone, the only people successfully to have resisted the Mongols at the height of their power. In the scroll, painted by a fighting man to claim rewards for his services, we see a lightly armed Japanese cavalryman on a spirited charger.

PLATE 37 – Haboku ('Splashed Ink') Landscape by Sesshū (1420–1506). Ink on paper. *147.3* ×
35.6 cm. National Museum, Tokyo. Cf. p. 167.

PLATE 38 – 'Storm on the Coast' by Sesson (1504–c. 1589). Ink on paper. *22.9* × *30.5 cm. Nomura Collection, Kyōtō. Cf. p. 168.*

PLATE 39 – 'Landscape' by Sō-ami (d. 1525). Ink and slight colours on paper. Daitoku-ji, Kyōtō. 175.3 × 121.9 cm. Cf. p. 168.

PLATE 40 – 'Stork on a Branch' by Kanō Motonobu (1476–1559). Ink and soft colour on paper. Reiun-in, Kyōtō. *50.8 × 118.1 cm. Cf. p. 169.*

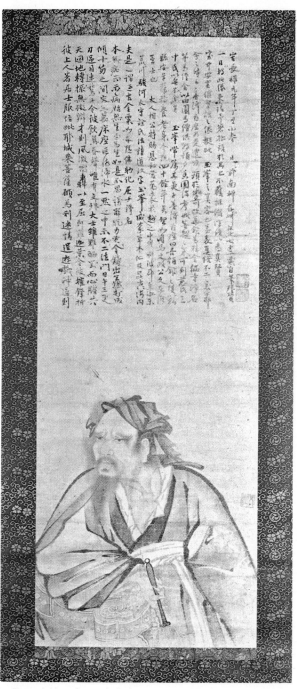

PLATE 41 – 'Yuima' by Bunsei (dated 1457). Ink on paper. Yamato Bunka-kan, Nara. *91.4 × 33 cm.*
Cf. p. 170.

PLATE 42 – 'Hinoki' (Pine-trees). Folding screen attributed to Kanō Eitoku (1543–90). Colour on gold paper. *168 × 456 cm. National Museum. Tokyo, Cf. p. 176.*

PLATE 43 – 'Pine-trees in the Mist' by Hasegawa Tōhaku (1539–1610). Pair of folding screens. Ink on paper. *Each screen 156 × 347 cm. National Museum, Tokyo. Cf. p. 177.*

PLATE 44 —"Flowers" by Hasegawa Tōhaku (1539-1610). Colour on paper. *Cf. p. 177f.*

Yet another side of the Japanese artistic character is revealed by a group of scrolls depicting the various illnesses to which man is heir and the various hells to which his soul may be consigned in the event of his leading a bad life, as well as the hungry ghosts which taunt it, there. The plate on page 112 shows a scene from the latter group, the Jigoku Sōshi or 'Hell Scrolls'. This depicts the Hell of Mortals and shows the particular fate awaiting those who steal from their fellow-men. Hell paintings are found in India and China and be-came popular in Japan from the eighth century onwards. Settled Fujiwara society, engrossed in its elegant life of pleasure, had little time for thoughts of hell, but the trials of inter-clan warfare and the fall of such eminent men as the Taira caused people to ponder on the ephemeral quality of life.

Buddhist cosmology teaches that there are Six Worlds of separate beings: the hells, that of hungry ghosts, of animals, of malevolent spirits, of human existence and of demi-gods. These contrast with the various worlds of the paradises — the Pure Land which was the only escape. It is a strange mixture of terror and humour.

During the Kamakura period Japanese ceramics proper began the long development which eventually raised them to a very accomplished and distinctive art. As one would expect, the wares of China, which had always dazzled the Japanese as they did the rest of the world, were the model. During the Sung period the Chinese raised the ceramic craft to a peak of artistic perfection which has never been surpassed. The celadon wares of Lung-ch'üan in Chekiang province and the *chien* wares of Fukien, the sombre black and brown glazes known in Japan as *temmoku*, were produced in large quanti-ties and exported to many countries as far away as the Middle East. But these fine products had well over a thousand years of develop-ment behind them and the Japanese could not hope to compete technically. What is more, the raw materials in the known sites of Japan were much inferior to those of China.

The Japanese claim that their ceramic craft was established during the Kamakura period by a certain Tōshirō, known as the 'father of Japanese pottery' — a tradition which some scholars view with scepticism. However, the tradition is correct from the point of view

FIGS. 48 to 53 – *Examples of old Seto ware with brown or yellow glazes. Cf. p. 146.*

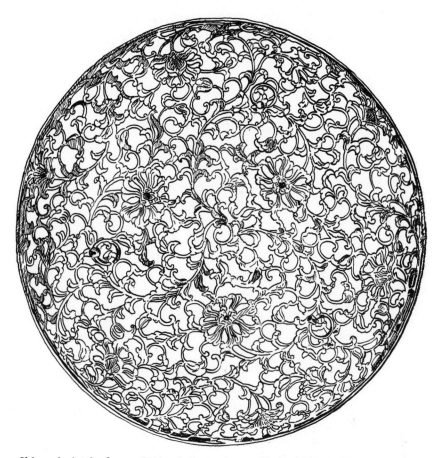

FIG. 54 – *Keko or basket for flowers. Gold and silver on bronze. Jinshō-ji Temple, Shiga. Diameter 28.8 cm. Cf. p. 146*

of time. The records state that Tōshirō went to China as a Buddhist priest and there studied the ceramic craft before returning to Japan about 1227–9 to establish a centre of manufacture in the Seto area. *Seto ware* About two hundred kilns dating from the Kamakura and the following Muromachi periods (1333–1572) have been discovered around Seto. Here in the thirteenth century the Japanese made their first high-fired wares or glazed stoneware. Seto is still the largest pottery-producing area in Japan and the word *seto-mono* or 'Seto-things' is often used for pottery in general.

The 'six old kilns of Japan' were: Seto, Tokoname, Shigaraki, Tamba, Bizen and Echizen. The last five produced the somewhat coarse pottery which with inverted sophistication the Japanese now appreciate very highly in their tea ceremonies; they will be discussed later. However, the Seto wares have a certain uniformity with their strong bold shapes, yellow, brown and black glazes, and incised or impressed designs. The new skill and variety in glazing was the result of the introduction of firing in oxidizing kilns instead of reducing kilns. Many of the pieces have a fine free-hand decoration and occasionally a fine crackle in the glaze. The glazes sometimes tend to streak in an attractive way. However, the Japanese could not approach the Chinese in ceramic skill and, with a few exceptions, the interest of these early pieces is historical rather than artistic.

FIGS. 48–53

METALWORK Generally speaking, the metalwork of the period continued Heian styles but with a tendency towards simpler forms and less ornate decoration than hitherto. In particular great attention was paid to swords and armour, both for their practical use and in their decoration. Some of the finest sword-blades ever made date to these centuries, although unfortunately this is an art which lies outside the competence of most Western historians. In iron tea-kettles and other Buddhist implements shapes began to acquire the classical lines brought over from Sung China. One remarkable piece of metalwork is illustrated in Figure 54 and this certainly recalls earlier craftsmanship in its involved delicacy. It is a basket used for scattering flowers in Buddhist ceremonies. Such baskets were usually made of bamboo but this example in gilt bronze is a masterpiece of metalwork. The design of open-work flowers is embellished with fine chiselling and emphasized by the use of both gold and silver plating. It recalls the delicacy of the metalwork on the Tamamushi shrine as well as a long line of distinguished objects in the same open-work technique produced by Japanese craftsmen over the centuries.

FIG. 54

PLATE P. 42

VII. THE ASHIKAGA OR MUROMACHI PERIOD
(1338–1573)

The period from 1272 to 1380 was one of very unsettled political *Decline of Kamakura* conditions culminating in civil war. The main source of weakness was the deterioration in the authority of the Kamakura leaders. The single-minded discipline of Yoritomo had become a thing of the past and the Hōjō regents who followed him were men of lesser calibre. The Mongol invasions had weakened the vigour of the Kamakura rulers who proved unable to control unruly elements in the provinces and the capital. They completely lost the initiative in the direction of national affairs and the resolution to shape their own destiny. The outcome of this was a movement to eliminate the dictators and restore the power of the throne—the customary and usually ineffective panacea for Japan in times of trouble.

Emperor Gō-Daigō ascended the throne in Kyōtō in 1318 — a man of 30 determined to put an end to cloister rule and make himself emperor in deed as well as in name. He obtained increasing support throughout the country, partly through his own real merits and partly through the greed of provincial lords who eyed with envy the fat landholdings which the Hōjō regents had accumulated. The Kamakura leaders could scarcely control the numerous uprisings throughout the country and, when the emperor with obvious popular support escaped from exile in 1333, the stage was set for a radical change.

The instrument of this change was to be Ashikaga Takauji, one of *Ashikaga Takauji* the most able and trusted of the Kamakura generals, who had been sent to capture the returned Emperor Gō-Daigō. Instead of obeying orders he defected to the imperial side, turned on the Kamakura stronghold in Kyōtō, captured it and re-established the emperor. Kamakura itself fell in July 1333 and all the Kamakura outposts in Kyūshū and elsewhere in the same year. The speed with which this happened showed the inner weakness of the Kamakura regents and the timeliness of the change.

Unfortunately the newly-restored emperor, although forming a splendid rallying point for discontented factions, for one reason or another proved inadequate as an administrator and failed to retain his supporters' loyalty. He broke the promises he had made them in harder times and was unable to share out fairly the spoils obtained from the Hōjō downfall. Bribery for favours was rife, and the worthy but unmannerly country warriors were not always successful in outwitting the court sycophants. Even the nobles became dissatisfied with Gō-Daigō, while the clergy outmatched the rest in their rapacity and treated the farming population most harshly. In fact the restoration seemed to have pleased nobody and anarchy was imminent. The emperor had failed to control the development of military power in the provinces and in such unsettled times it was understandable that many people looked back to the days of firm Kamakura leadership when they felt that they had at least been fairly governed. In such a time of crisis the country showed a growing impatience with the stupid trivia of court ceremonial which seemed to absorb the energies of men who should have been using them to administer and restore the country. In such circumstances it was left to Takauji to seize power. He killed his main opponent, the emperor's son, and when the emperor himself was goaded into action, he defeated him and took control. By the end of 1336 he was master of the old capital and seemingly of Japan, while the emperor found himself, as many times before and after, once more subordinate to a general. Takauji obviously considered himself as the logical successor to the leaders of the feudal order.

Civil war However, Takauji's temporary victory by no means solved the problems facing Japan and the influence of the throne was not eradicated. For no less than fifty-six years a struggle was waged between a puppet emperor called Kōmyō from the senior imperial line, who was put on the throne in Kyōtō by Takauji, and Emperor Gō-Daigō and his successors, who fled and established their seat at Yoshino, a mountain fastness in the south. This long period of civil war is known as the Namboku-chō, 'the Northern and Southern Courts'; it produced many notable men and some of the most heroic moments in Japanese history.

FIG. 55 – *Kinkaku-ji, Kyōtō. Cf. p. 150.*

The loyalists in the south proved extremely tenacious and difficult to root out. Takauji's position was by no means secure and he experienced considerable opposition from some of his own supporters, who could see no reason for continuing any association whatsoever with an imperial line. In the constant fighting Kyōtō changed hands several times. Takauji himself died in 1358 aged fifty-four, having spent twenty-six years in almost constant campaigning. He was succeeded by his own son Yoshiakira, and then in 1368 by the nine-year-old Yoshimitsu. It was not until 1383 that, after fierce fighting, the Kyūshū strongholds of the southern court were finally subdued. By 1392 the Ashikaga had established their supremacy over both the southern court and their own more recalcitrant warriors. In an atmosphere of exhaustion a union of the two imperial lines was effected and, after some very shady treatment of the southern emperor, the northern line was supreme.

Rise of warrior class During the course of the civil war the powerful and warlike barons further increased their power, and as a result there developed a military rather than a feudal society. The Kyōtō nobility lost whatever authority they had once possessed and in the wars new men from the provinces came to the fore bearing names which survived down to recent times. Moreover, the absence of so many leaders of provincial society for long periods on campaigns gave the more able members of the farming community an opportunity to secure more independence than they had hitherto enjoyed. As Sansom points out, one of the most remarkable tributes to Japanese culture is the fact that, during this period of about a hundred years of almost incessant fighting, the aristocracy was able to preserve the traditional Japanese interest in the arts and letters. The Ashikaga shōguns, while seeming to degrade the emperor, felt it natural to assume his mantle as supporters of the arts. Yoshimitsu in particular was an extravagant builder and an enthusiastic supporter of the theatre. His palace in the Muromachi quarter of Kyōtō has given the period one of the names by which it is often known, the 'Muro-

FIG. 55 machi period'. The graceful Kinkaku-ji or 'Golden Pavilion' which he built for his retirement is one of the most famous edifices in Kyōtō and all Japan. More of a summer palace than a temple, it is poised lightly over a lake almost ethereal in its grace. However, the taxes he imposed for his expensive rebuilding programme were a heavy burden on an impoverished people and both he and his vassals were forced to turn to trade with China to replenish their treasuries. The long civil war had exhausted the Ashikaga and they had little strength left to consolidate their power. In fact they remained in control only because there was no other leader strong enough to assume the overlordship.

Growing influence
of Zen Nevertheless, after the long civil war the country was ready to accept the blessings of peace even if it did have to pay somewhat dearly for them. Zen priests became popular and powerful in the

150

highest quarters. We have seen how the sect entered Japan in strength during the Kamakura period. The Chinese for Zen is Ch'an, a transliteration of the Sanskrit word *dhyāna*, which can be partially translated as 'meditation'. The Indian missionary Bodhidharma, who brought the sect to China in A.D. 520, himself summarized the teaching as follows: 'A special transmission outside the scriptures. No dependence on words and letters. Pointing directly to the heart (or intuitive mind) of man. Seeing into one's own nature and the attainment of Buddhahood'. For man the essential awakening comes through introspection and sudden enlightenment. All the other trappings of religion were useless. In former times the sect demanded strict discipline and frugality, which appealed to those with early Kamakura standards. The Zen priests were the natural leaders of learning and culture; since they were more familiar than anyone else with what was going on in China after the establishment of the Ming dynasty in 1368, they provided advisers in foreign affairs. Contacts with the mainland improved rapidly. They were naturally anxious to re-establish contact with their brethren in China, and the Japanese in general were eager for the benefits of trade, whether by legitimate means or piracy. The Chinese were equally happy to trade with the Japanese, although they of course affected to treat them and the embassies under which they masqueraded as traditional 'tributaries'. The Japanese exchanged swords, horses, paper, lacquer and bronze for Chinese silk, books, drugs, porcelain and art works of all kinds, particularly paintings. However, these relations varied greatly in intensity and trade was often in the hands of pirates who proved a scourge of the Chinese coastal areas. Nevertheless, there is no doubt that the quality and tasteful design of many Japanese products made them highly sought after in China. One result of this thriving trade was the emergence of a virile merchant class, which was to prove most important for Japan's later development. Around the provincial lords there grew up a new class of mercenaries: the *rōnin* or 'wave men', *samurai* without land or master who earned their living by the sword. Legends concerning the exploits of these men enriched the lore of Japan and provided stimulating material for literature and art.

Contact with mainland expanded

In this politically decadent atmosphere the arts flourished. Local lords, striving to emulate the manners and luxury of Kyōtō, welcomed men of art and letters whether priests or not. In the Ashikaga period, under teachers like Musō, the standards of personal life for Zen monks relaxed; priests formed a taste for luxury and for the benefits of high living, masked by bogus poverty. As many critics have pointed out, although Zen adherents professed to despise the written word as coming between them and enlightenment, this did not stop them from writing tomes on the subject. But the Zen faith had a wide and deep influence on the arts — especially on that of painting. Zen painters saw the speed with which an artist with brush and ink could communicate his vision as an example of the flash of enlightenment following proper meditation.

Equally they claimed that the Buddhahood or truth could be seen in even the most seemingly trivial aspect of nature — a twig of a tree, a falling blossom, a grain of sand. This search for the divine underlying every aspect of the myriad phenomena of the world about us enriched the scope, deepened the appreciation and sharpened the sensitivity of generations of artists. Through it the Far East made one of its greatest contributions to the art of the world.

SCULPTURE The great period of sculpture seems to have ended with the Kamakura era. It is difficult to understand precisely why the stream of creative talent in this field seems to have dried up so quickly and suddenly. Perhaps the Japanese followed the Chinese in this respect, for by the Ming dynasty (1368–1644) no new contribution was being made to this art in China itself. Ming sculpture is, generally speaking, either a degradation of the mellifluous lines of Sung or heavy, rather stolid figures in T'ang style from which all life and movement is missing. The great age of Buddhism was rapidly waning in China and no new impulses came to revive it. Ch'an (Zen) Buddhism had removed the *raison d'être* for statues of deities, and from this time onwards Japanese carvers seem to have devoted themselves increasingly to miniature works; later this resulted in a flood of exquisite decorative articles, such as *netsuke* buttons, in a wide range of materials and of infinite ingenuity. The temples were no longer the great patrons of the ateliers as they had been in the past. The local leaders seem to have lost interest in the temples, while the merchants, who were later to take over the role of patrons, looked elsewhere for artistic rewards for their new wealth. These understandably took the form of personal and household adornments. As the cultural leaders turned more to painting, so also did the wealthy classes who copied them.

The main interest of art in this period centres on painting. This was strongly under the influence of the work imported from China, particularly the monochrome work of the Sung and early Ming dynasties (10th–15th century). The Ashikaga shōguns set the pattern for this renewed addiction to things Chinese, notably the eighth shōgun, Yoshimasa, whose catalogue of Chinese paintings was written by Sō-ami (see below). The old colourful Japanese style fell out of favour, although its main practitioners, the Tosa school, continued to produce many attractive narrative scrolls inspired by the old manners. Generally speaking, however, the new monochrome *Minchō* ink landscape styles took command. The 'Hermitage by a Mountain Brook' attributed to Minchō (Chō Densu) (A.D. 1352–1431) is a typical early example of the Japanese enslavement to the new PLATE P. 113 Chinese ideals. Like many outstanding painters of the period, Minchō combined artistic taste with religious duties. The style is a faithful echo of a Sung landscape tradition, a combination of strong brushwork and a theme which appealed equally to both intellectual and romantic sentiments. An area of water with a hut perched above it, mist-shrouded mountains in the background, a few rocks — this is the perfect union of intellectual repose and romantic surroundings which has coloured our vision of Far Eastern life. The dream is that of the Chinese scholar-administrator, of escape from the bonds of everyday life to the peace of the countryside. There, in communion with friends, a man of contemplative nature can enjoy the grandeur of nature and its underlying order. The appeal to us in the twentieth century is irresistible.

Everything about the picture is strictly Chinese in taste but, even as early as this, the softer misty landscape of Japan has left its mark on the artist's interpretation. Minchō had never been to China itself and his inspiration, attractive though it is, is second-hand. The style is a mixture of those which came out of China, with an emphasis on academy work as developed in early Ming. As in Chinese works many poems and writings decorate the painting itself and emphasize the literary connection and connotation. In seeking out the Japanese characteristics, one may say that there is perhaps a contrived air about the painting, a somewhat self-conscious approach to Chinese technique, but it is difficult to be more specific. As one might expect, the general treatment is marked by a tendency to gloss over areas not understood in favour of emphasis on the main elements. It is not possible to say that this is necessarily the failing of the copyist, for it is a characteristic of Japanese art which has produced some of its most original achievements.

Kaō

PLATE P. 114 The imaginary portrait of Kanzan by Kaō illustrates a number of the tendencies of the period. Kaō was both a Zen priest and a painter but, apart from this scant information, we know very little of his life or background. Some say that his work spanned the late Kamakura and early Muromachi periods, which makes him one of the earliest ink painters. The subject is a Chinese Zen priest, one of a pair of seemingly simple-minded prelates of the T'ang dynasty (A.D. 618–907), known in Japanese as Kanzan and Jittoku. They are probably quite apocryphal figures who, according to the tradition which has grown up around them, discarded the intellectual and presumptuous attitudes of the other sects. Content at having discovered enlightenment, they felt free to ignore the benefits of worldly comfort. Such pairs of portraits were a popular theme for ink painters through the centuries both in China and Japan. They are, of course, in their way as real and as didactic as any more formal icon.

Kaō's work is distinguished by its economy of brushwork and powerful line. The flat-footed figure gapes at some unseen spectacle. Pot-bellied and ragged, he stands in vacuous good humour detached from the world. Part of a tree in soft washes echoes the stance and the approach is as unselfconscious as the brushwork itself. The painting and its message is a tilt at convention, with the added humour which leavens much of Japanese art at all times. As an icon it is carefully calculated to administer the maximum shock to the convert seeking religious enlightenment. Such paintings, like so many early works in the medium, are very close to their Chinese prototypes; were they not signed it would take a brave historian to distinguish them.

The painting 'Catfish and Gourd' summarizes a number of the tendencies of the early Ashikaga period. It was painted by Josetsu, about whom very little is known apart from the fact that he was acknowledged to be the greatest teacher of the age. He was probably a priest-painter and a member of the Zen sect. He worked for the Ashikaga shōgunate. Above the painting itself are thirty inscriptions by Zen priests of the period 1394–1427. This practice, so strange to Western custom, is characteristic of Far Eastern painting. Sometimes these added inscriptions are by the artist himself and give autobiographical information or the source of his inspiration for the painting; sometimes they are poems or lines of appreciation by friends or connoisseurs inspired by it at the time when it was painted or later. It appears from one of these that the Ashikaga shōgun ordered the painting for a screen and that he asked for the work to be done in the 'new style'. Thus we see how the new rulers of Japan were ready to act as patrons of art very soon after they came into power and that they were enthralled by the vogue for Chinese styles. *Josetsu* PLATE P. 115

The elements of the composition are very simple: a stream with a few rocks, a bamboo and a few reeds in the foreground, and the merest suggestion of foliage on misty hills in the background. The attention is entirely centered on the tattered priest in the foreground who is trying to catch a slippery catfish in a gourd. This is a representation of a typical Zen 'impossibility' which is claimed to stimulate the student to enlightenment. The intimate style is that of the Southern Sung period and again there is nothing to distinguish it as a Japanese rather than a Chinese painting except that no Chinese painting has survived with a similar subject. Intellectually the Japanese seem to have identified themselves completely with Chinese culture. But, unlike the earlier period, now they did so feeling themselves to be fully equal. After the centuries of isolation and internal disorder the new artistic developments in China must have come as a revelation, but the Japanese rose to the challenge of this new art with amazing speed and facility.

Shūbun Another excellent illustration of the extremely difficult problem of distinguishing early Japanese landscapes in the Chinese style from those of China is the 'Studio of the Three Worthies' in the Seikadō PLATE P. 116 Foundation, Tokyo. Like a number of similar early landscapes it is attributed to Shūbun, who was active in the first half of the fifteenth century. He was a pupil of Josetsu and probably the teacher of the greatest of all ink painters, Sesshū (see below). He seems to have been familiar with the Ashikaga shōgun's collections of Chinese paintings, many of which, if the Japanese echoes are valid, must have been in the early Ming style as inherited from such Southern Sung court masters as Ma Yüan and Hsia Kuei. The ideal vision of nature which this style presents, and which is repeated down the centuries with almost monotonous regularity, is explained by Paine as 'The amalgamation of Buddhism and Confucian philosophy... most apparent in landscape paintings. Art embodying this philosophy of nature gave to every selected detail a pre-established value. Indestructible mountain ranges weather out the everchanging seasons. Man is depicted as one who searches for, finds, and fills himself with natural purity. Mountain, tree and man bear a definite proportion. Atmosphere is used to suggest by shifting areas of mist a sense of distance so extensive in height and width that what first seems a naturalistic panorama becomes a cosmic view, pulsating with the energy of life itself. The beauty of nature thus intellectually conceived reflects the profundity of Chinese thought about nature by the measure of ideal forms. The tradition is as distinctive a contribution to art history as the ideal proportions with which the Greeks represented the physique of man.'[1]

It is again interesting to try to isolate the specifically Japanese quality in such a painting. Perhaps it is too clear-cut; it is a little too 'pat', with elements of mannerism creeping in much as they do in inflated Ming dynasty landscapes in the Sung style. The brushwork is impeccable. Depth and atmospheric effects are all perfectly worked out, but an indefinable lack of reality produces a dream-like quality which is not so evident in Sung landscapes.

[1] R. T. Paine and A. Soper, *The Art and Architecture of Japan* (London 1955), p. 82.

The greatest artist of the period was certainly a priest named
Sesshū (1420–1506) who went to China in the mid-Ming period
(1468–69) where, it is said, he was so successful that he was offered
the headship of a great Chinese monastery. Chinese academic paint-
ing at this time was suffering from exhaustion and lack of inspira-
tion, and Sesshū with his powerful brushwork had indeed something
new to offer even to the Chinese. In the first place he knew what
the Chinese countryside really looked like and therefore he had no
need to reproduce from others' work. By the time that Sesshū was
active he was of course thoroughly familiar with the long landscape
scroll from similar paintings of the Sung dynasty. The Japanese
were also familiar with the scroll format from the splendid painted
scrolls of the Kamakura period, in long passages of which landscapes
form the background to stories of the lives and deeds of monks. Two
such scrolls completely in the Chinese manner have survived from
Sesshū: the 'Longer Landscape Scroll' which, in all, is about fifty-
two feet in length, and the 'Landscape of the Four Seasons', of
which the 'Winter Landscape' is here given as an illustration. The
reproduction of only a single section can hardly be expected to do
justice to the sustained inspiration and the variations in mood which
an artist can depict within a scroll. As has often been pointed out,
such landscape scrolls differ from Western landscape painting in
that they add the time element to the art of painting. The work is
entirely Chinese in inspiration, and it would be difficult to dis-
tinguish it from a Chinese painting were it not for its very clear-cut,
powerful brushwork and the tendency to schematization in the
background mountains. The Japanese have a liking for minute
observation of small details and for assembling them into a large
unit. The Chinese, however, tend rather to look at nature and
synthesize. The Japanese approach in most cases is more intimate
for that reason, and consequently the grandeur of Chinese landscape
is often reduced. In the stark scene of his 'Winter Landscape'
Sesshū seems to have tried deliberately to simplify nature with a
few jagged brush-strokes.

The scene he paints is the depth of winter with its sharp contrasts
of black and white, a world in which the snow throws everything
into stark relief expressed in clear outlines and silhouettes. This is a

Sesshū

PLATE P. 117

skeletal world in which a bowed figure slowly makes its way towards the snow-covered roofs of a distant village. Here Sesshū has pushed the Chinese style to its limit by thickening the ink and emphasizing the line to a degree never attempted by the Chinese. A nervous vitality runs through it, as it does through much of the most Japanese of Japanese painting in Chinese monochrome ink styles. Above all, the softness of the Sung prototype has been ruthlessly cut away and the weakness of the Ming traditionalists injected with new virility amounting almost to violence. The trap into which many Japanese painters fell was that of mistaking technical ability for artistic power. It is a style which is only too easy to follow but at the risk of sacrificing the qualities which save it from sentimentality on the one hand and technical exhibitionism on the other. However, Sesshū, unlike many of his contemporaries, was not an artistic snob in that he would only paint Chinese landscapes, real or imaginary. He was a true Japanese in his appreciation of the countryside of his native land; oddly enough, he was one of the first painters to realize that one could legitimately apply the lessons of Chinese monochrome painting to the land of his birth.

PLATE P. 118 Sesshū's 'Ama-no-Hashidate', one of the 'Three Scenic Beauty Spots of Japan' in the plate on page 118 is a view from high up of one of the favourite places in the Japanese islands, typical in its rounded volcanic hills, covered with soft vegetation, and little inlets, each one explored and frequented for its delicate beauty. Such landscapes have the compressed quality of a Japanese garden in the same way that the English countryside so often looks like a park where nature has been artfully improved on. The three planes are skilfully connected by the water with its busy traffic. The small scale has curbed the boldness of his line and the steamy atmosphere of summer covers the background in soft tones. The eye is tempted to climb the mountain path up towards the hamlet clustering in the crown of its summit. To add interest the artist names the important temples and shrines. Scholars have proved that he painted this, perhaps a sketch for a final version since lost, when he was over eighty. One feels that it could well be only a section of a long scroll in the grandest manner recording a journey down the coast of Japan.

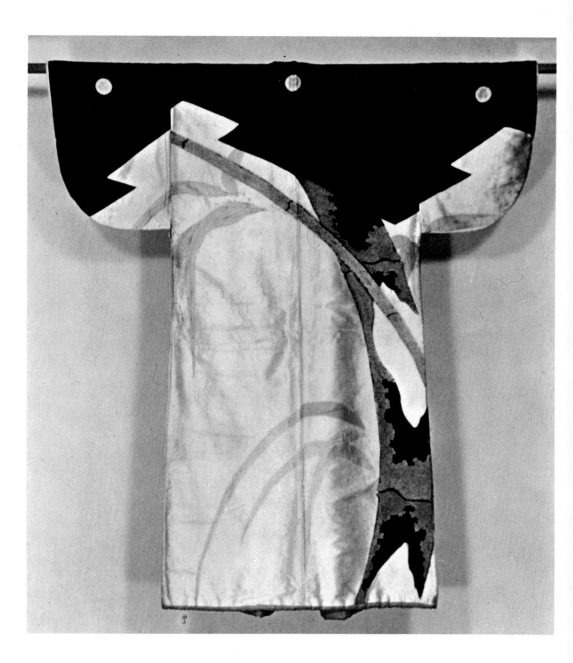

PLATE 45 – Short-sleeved robe (*kosode*). Decorated with design of bamboo on a white and purple background. Daihiko Senshū Bijutsu Kenkyūjō, Tokyo. *Height 144.9 cm. Cf. p. 180.*

PLATE 46 – Namban-byōbu ('Southern Barbarian' screen). Arrival of a Portuguese ship and welcoming of a group of Jesuits. Anonymous. 17th cent. *154.2 × 565.2 cm. Kobayashi Collection, Tokyo. Cf. p. 179.*

PLATE 47 – Decorated or painted Karatsu-ware jar. Early 17th cent. *Cf. p. 182.*

PLATE 48 – Typical *raku*-ware tea-bowl. 16th–17th cents. *Cf. p. 191.*

PLATE 49 – One of a pair of screens, 'Sekiya' ('The Barrier Hut') by Tawaraya Sōtatsu (active *c.* 1596–1623). Colour on paper. Early 17th cent. *157 × 263 cm. Seikadō Foundation, Tokyo. Cf. p. 196.*

PLATE 50 – One of a pair of folding screens, 'Red and White Plum-trees' by Ōgata Kōrin (1658–1716). Colour on gold paper. *Each screen 166 × 172 cm. Atami Museum, Shizuoka. Cf. p. 198.*

PLATE 51 – Sliding door with landscape painted in ink on paper (?) by Yōsa Buson (1716–83). *Museum of Eastern Art, Cologne. Cf. p. 199.*

One cannot leave Sesshū without mention of one of the greatest ink landscapes produced by the whole Far Eastern ink tradition: his 'Haboku' or 'Splashed Ink' Landscape in the Tokyo National Museum. Here the artist has dispensed with the strong outlines he used in his more familiar landscape style; a few seemingly hasty splashes and washes of ink in various tones appear to explode like a shellburst into a misty landscape with trees, huts and towering mountains in the background. No twentieth-century artist ever abstracted the elements of landscape more completely. PLATE P. 135

The technique is Chinese in origin and one which had been developing from the T'ang dynasty. It was much favoured by the Zen painters because it enabled them to illustrate in brush and ink the kind of process which might lead to spiritual enlightenment. There is an element of magic in such apparently spontaneous creativeness which appealed to their philosophy, and the seeming simplicity and frugality of the means made an irresistible appeal. The composition is masterly in the way it plays off the violent foreground against the calm, almost hidden mountains. The tiny figure in the boat provides an important key to the scale and introduces a telling human element. This technique is extremely difficult to achieve convincingly. It is interesting to note that Sesshū had very little good to say of the artistic talents of his contemporaries in China when he stayed there, but he recorded how grateful he was to have been able at least to learn this particular technique. The result is both expressionistic and highly dramatic. In the direction of these two qualities lies the Japanese contribution to ink painting. The nervous brush of the Japanese painter adds this explosive ingredient which is rarely found in Chinese painting; but the danger for the Japanese is to overdo it and enjoy the technique for its own sake — a skill which perhaps belongs more to calligraphy than to painting. It is perhaps unfair to reproduce in a survey of this scope four works by one master, but Sesshū is certainly one of the artistic giants of Japanese painting who both embodies many of the artistic elements of his own time and anticipates those that came later. He had a foot in two different worlds and worked at a time when the Japanese artist was beginning to appreciate this ambivalence. He was conscious of the innovations of the age, of the achievements of China but also of the call of his own heritage. He knew he could surpass his Chinese contemporaries in their own field and at the same time awaken his countrymen to the beauties of their own landscape. He was never timid and a stirring boldness runs through his works, all of which carry the stamp of individuality and confidence. His art is securely rooted in the traditions of China but it breathes the spirit of the Japanese temperament.

Sesson

A small painting done in the wake of Sesshū develops the ink tradition as seen at the end of the period. Sesson (1504–*c.* 1589) lived and worked away from the main artistic centre of Kyōtō. His powerful 'Storm on the Coast' exploits fully the powerful economy possible

PLATE P. 136

in ink painting but adds an atmosphere and movement which in its violence is rare in Chinese painting. He seems to have appreciated the fury of the elements more than the Chinese. A puny boat with fragile sails runs before the wind. Swathes of rain and light sweep across the scene, angry waves reach out to dash themselves against the rocks. The whole direction of the movement is in a diagonal from top right to bottom left and all the elements — trees, bamboo, boat and hut — brace themselves in different ways but all determined to withstand the onslaught. This is not an intellectual landscape studied from the Chinese but a personal experience dramatically set down with consistent vision and assured technique.

Sō-ami

It is not a very far step from the work of Sesshū and Minchō to that of the 'Three Amis', Nō-ami (1397–1471), his son Gei-ami (1431–95) and his grandson Sō-ami (1472–1525), whom we mentioned as the author of the catalogue of Ashikaga paintings. Sō-ami was enamoured of the landscape painters of South China. These men painted quiet, misty landscapes in which the outlines are softened by haze and cloud. It was a type of scenery more familiar to the

PLATE P. 137

Japanese and met with a ready response. The landscape in the plate on page 137 once formed part of some sliding doors and was only later remounted as a hanging scroll. It is of classical South Chinese inspiration, with wing-like hills reaching out into the central area and with banks of mist effecting the transition from foreground to middle distance and then to background. The eye is led effortlessly to follow the receding landscape. A few peasants and travellers around a settlement extol the rustic life, a temple emerges from the pines. In much of the work of the 'Three Amis' the brushwork is forced and the rhythms too consciously formulated, but here Sō-ami has produced a genuinely atmospheric scene painted with gentle sensitivity. Even the size has not ruined the touch.

The Zen-inspired landscapes of the period constitute one of the peaks of Japanese painting. As the period progressed the religious inspiration tended to disappear, yielding to the ever strong Japanese sense of decoration. This took place in the works of the Kanō school *Kanō school* which increasingly dominated the artistic scene until, as we shall see later in the Tokugawa period, it became the 'official school', patronized by the court and by all who had cultural aspirations. The founder of the school was Kanō Masanobu (*c.* 1435–1530), a contemporary of Sesshū, and the fortunes of the school were firmly established by Kanō Motonobu (1476–1559). The family produced generation after generation of able painters — some genuine members of the family and some, in good Eastern fashion, promising apprentices adopted in order to keep the family name alive.

From the first the members of the Kanō school were not priests and therefore felt themselves free to dispense with the religious content. However, the Buddhist element was often displaced by a Confucian moralizing element which reflects the popularity of Confucian thought following its victory in China. The Kanō were called on to carry out large-scale decorations of rooms in the new palaces. The 'Stork on a Branch' in the plate on page 138 is one of forty-nine PLATE P. 138 'Landscapes with Flowers and Birds' which Motonobu did to decorate the Reiun-in, a temple in Kyōtō. It was painted on a *fusuma* or sliding screen and has now been mounted as a hanging scroll to protect it.

The painting has no great pretensions or religious overtones. A soft elegant bird perches on a gnarled pine-branch over water. A few decorative waves beneath him and the mist are intended to suggest the lonely space beyond, but in a facile way compared with Chinese Sung landscapes. All the elements are thoroughly familiar from Chinese painting, not to say clichés, and the genuine depth of feeling has disappeared. The painter does not approach his subject with humility but, as a decorator should, with boldness and confidence. He works from the outside rather than from the inside; the aim is purely decorative, demanding clarity of expression rather than subtlety of emotion. Stylization takes the place of inner life. One must judge this type of painting by completely different standards from those of Chinese painting. In its genre it ranks among the world's most striking and artistic forms of decoration. One is expected to appreciate the power of brushwork and the boldness of conception. The Japanese admire the sense of daring in such works, the expression of a powerful personality and the way in which such a painting dominates the room.

The Japanese gift for portraiture was continued in the portrait of the Disciple of the Buddha known as Yuima (Sanskrit: Vimalakīrti),

PLATE P. 139 a popular theme for both Chinese and Japanese painting. Yuima, according to Buddhist tradition, was a lay follower of the Buddha who refused to become a priest and is often depicted in religious argument with the Bodhisattva Monju (Manjushrī). In this instance a priest ordered a religious painter of the Daitoku-ji, Kyōtō, to paint the portrait of the saint in the image of his father, who had

Bunsei been a *samurai* . The painter was Bunsei (mid-15th century), who was also famed for his landscapes in the Chinese style; the work is dated 1457. Many portraits of Zen priests have survived, but most of them follow a somewhat rigid pattern in which the prelate is shown seated stiffly on a large chair. Since the Zen sect set little store by icons and religious illustrations, this type of portraiture was a popular outlet for artistic talents. This figure of Yuima is quite unlike the formal Zen portraits in its power and freedom. Its vigorous animation is typically Japanese, and the heavy outlines of the robes reveal the Japanese brush as unmistakably as they do in the many imaginary portraits of Bodhidharma. Seldom has a Japanese artist succeeded so well in blending naturalism and idealism. Its effect comes from a combination of virility, solemnity and simplicity in composition combined with faultless brushwork. The Japanese developed the dramatic feeling in such portraits in a most personal way.

The Zen beliefs had a considerable effect on the art of tea, or the tea ceremony as it is known. Tea was introduced by Chinese monks, and their Japanese colleagues found it had qualities as a mild stimulant which suited the life of the monk. It was said to induce harmony, reverence, purity and tranquillity, the essential ingredients of the priestly community. Hardly a building could be made without its tea room — small, tasteful and austere, with all its decoration and construction conducive to meditation. There differences of rank was levelled, intellectual talk encouraged and artistic appreciation the order. The tea-bowls themselves are powerful in their simplicity, never far removed from the clay of which they are made and often showing the marks of potters' hands. The other implements and accoutrements are chosen to set each other off; a fine piece of silk, a humble iron pot. At its best this sophisticated primitiveness has an evocative charm and the early tea-masters were sensitive arbiters of taste. At its worst it is one of the most contrived ceremonies on earth. Certainly it has stimulated an appreciation in Japan of quiet good taste, encouraged men to dwell for a moment on the qualities of even the most humble object and to ponder on the essence of beauty.

Rise of warrior class   The Ashikaga period witnessed many changes in Japanese society. During the long wars there rose to power a new class of warriors, men of much humbler origin than those who had hitherto ruled the country. Distinguished by their military prowess, they displaced the older families and made themselves masters of large areas. For the first time ability rather than heredity became the essential criterion for high office. The new rulers built up their following by a mixture of fair government and firm discipline enforced through harsh punishment of those who infringed their will. The recipe was much the same as that of the early Kamakura leaders. Their fair treatment of the peasants won for them the support of this class of Japanese society, which had hitherto suffered badly at the hands of all who held sway over them. This was a new element in Japanese politics. The new warrior class built themselves huge castles, sometimes seven storeys high, which rose gracefully from massive curving stone

FIG. 56   walls. It is a proof of the ingrained love of learning and the arts in the East that these rough warriors, without the benefits of hereditary culture, immediately strove to make these places centres of culture, welcoming poets and often employing resident artists. Those among them who engaged in the China trade were particularly interested in the arts and as a result Kyōtō became less than hitherto the only place in Japan which enjoyed a full artistic life.

Nobunaga   The man who inaugurated the Momoyama period was typical of the new leaders. Oda Nobunaga (1534–82) came from a family which had been relatively obscure in the fifteenth century. He was only twenty when he became head of his family in 1551 and at first his position was strongly disputed. But by 1559 his courage and determination made him the unchallenged leader of his clan and master of Echizen province. The following year he defeated his nearest rival and neighbour Imagawa, and was well placed geo-graphically to control Kyōtō, which was situated immediately across the waist of the country. Nobunaga strengthened his position by marriage and warfare; in this he was well supported by two able generals, Tokugawa Ieyasu and Toyotomi Hideyoshi, who were destined to carry on his work. It was not long before the enfeebled Ashikaga Shōgun Yoshiaki, hard-pressed by the insubordinate warriors around him, called on Nobunaga for support. He respond-ed promptly and restored Yoshiaki to power. Nobunaga first re-spected or pretended to respect the shōgun and the emperor alike but Yoshiaki, thinking perhaps that he was only another upstart, proved unreliable; in 1573 Nobunaga took the logical step and deposed him. Indeed, once a new leader with sufficient power emerged the Ashikaga were superfluous.

Nobunaga then proceeded to crush any actual or potential chal-lengers, and this he did with a ruthlessness that was severe even by Japanese standards of the day. He set about the task of bringing his fellow barons under control and put down the war-like monks in the temple strongholds of Mount Hiei and other places. Those at Ōsaka proved to be the most difficult to subdue and only acknow-ledged defeat after a ten-year siege. Nobunaga was finally assassi-nated by a discontented general in 1582, leaving his lieutenant, Hideyoshi, to complete his work. The latter overwhelmed the south

Hideyoshi

of Kyūshū Island by 1587 and the undisciplined north by 1590. Further resistance seemed useless.

Hideyoshi, the 'Napoleon of Japan', died in 1598 and the last seventeen years of the Momoyama period were taken up with Tokugawa Ieyasu's struggle to inherit the seat of power and organize the country so that he and his successors could keep possession of it. The Momoyama period lasted less than half a century but it laid the foundations of modern Japan and paved the way for two hun-dred and fifty years of peace in the ensuing Tokugawa period.

Having achieved supreme power, Hideyoshi was faced with the problem of occupying his armies, which had numbered as many as a quarter of a million men. He chose a programme of foreign adventure. The trade with China had shown how much profit there was to be had from that country, and Hideyoshi even contemplated an attack on the mainland. The Ming dynasty was now in decline, and collapsed half a century later in 1644. But his choice fell on Korea, which he invaded in 1592 and 1597–8. The second campaign was cut short by Hideyoshi's death in 1598 and Tokugawa Ieyasu took over. The campaigns were an almost total failure.

Castle-building The Momoyama or 'Peach Hill' period is named after a castle of that name which Hideyoshi built in 1593. Another of Nobunaga's castles situated on the shores of beautiful Lake Biwa near Kyōtō was destroyed in 1582 after his death. The largest, which Hideyoshi built at Ōsaka, perished in 1615. The best known is the Shirasagi FIG. 56 or 'White Heron' castle at Himeji, which has recently been restored; it is also one of the most graceful. It dates to the end of the sixteenth century and was expanded in 1608–9. A large seven-storeyed tower rises about 100 feet on granite walls with smaller four- or five-storeyed keeps, a unique combination of the elegance and strength which often provide the main ingredients of all Momoyama art. Unfortunately such castles were rapidly made obsolete as military strongholds by the firearms introduced by the Portuguese, who at this time were beginning to enter Japan as missionaries.

PAINTING Nevertheless these castles provided the setting and set the tone for the period. The warlords spared no expense to lighten and brighten their interiors with an art of splendid buoyancy and brilliance — a decorative art which has no equal. Like many parvenus, these men were determined to add to their spoils all the rewards of power — the luxuries of elegant living and art to match their colourful and vivid lives. The gusto of their age is reflected in a restless seeking for invention and originality such as one finds in Italy during the early sixteenth century. But whereas the human figure and the requirements of naturalism to some extent held Western artists in check, the Japanese were free to experiment with form and colour almost without restraint. Only a tree or some other object from nature provide any kind of reference to reality.

Eitoku Kanō Eitoku (1543–90), grandson of Motonobu, was the spokesman of this early 'modern period' in Japanese art; it was he whom

Nobunaga and Hideyoshi chose to decorate their new castles. Eitoku contributed the sliding screens to the Juraku Palace, the 'Mansion of Pleasure', a building of unrivalled magnificence constructed in Kyōtō by Hideyoshi in 1587. In 1591 he gave this to his nephew and with a reported fifty thousand men built in a mere two months the Palace of Peace at Momoyama, 'Peach Hill', south of Kyōtō. The builders landscaped it in a park; the greatest artists of the time were ordered to decorate it and provide a setting worthy of the men of learning and letters whom Hideyoshi gathered around him. The palace perished by earthquake and fire not long after his death. The workmen who had created and decorated it dispersed to spread the new decorative ideals in many other centres.

Much of Eitoku's work has been lost and it is therefore difficult to form a complete view of his contribution. However, the screen in the plate on page 140 shows his style fully formed. The pivot of this brilliant design is a huge gnarled tree-trunk from which one snake-like arm reaches out to touch and hold the farthest panel. A deep blue sea with rocks and thick banks of billowing clouds, cleverly arranged to throw the aged tree into sharp contrast, complete a powerful composition which can have few parallels in the art of decoration. Only a few leaves are shown, not enough to break up the bold outlines. With its bold verticals and horizontals the composition has a simple basis. The taste is frankly bombastic, suited to the character of the new rulers of Japan who could not afford and were not in sympathy with the refinement of Ashikaga taste. Such art is a declared intention to improve on nature, to gild the lily. It attempts to bring the elements of landscape into the interior of the house in such a bold way as to overwhelm the spectator. An important element of modern Japanese design shows itself in the manner in which the landscape deliberately flows over the edge of the screen as if unwilling to recognize any restraint. The Far Eastern artists' ancient appeal to the spectator's imagination here finds a new formula which owes nothing to Chinese or Zen sensibilities.

Miniature objects Such screens provide in their grandest form the combination of art and nature which lies at the root of much later Japanese art, from a tea-bowl to a flower arrangement, from a colour-print to a garden. The miniature objects which are a constant source of delight spring from the same combination — gold on black in the lacquer, brilliant precious metals on base metals in a sword-guard. The Japanese artistic sense turned away from the discreet and subdued, from the implied and evocative, as if in revolt against the Chinese masters and their Japanese pupils. Colour and design became lavish and explicit. Vivid contrasts were expected and indeed made the impact. One wonders if they were not influenced by the textiles of the period which had steadily become bolder and more eye-catching (see page 179).

At the same time, technical changes were essential to deal with the new scale on which the artists were working. We hear that Eitoku used a brush made of straw in order to achieve the strength of brushwork he sought, much as some modern calligraphers do. But even in this highly individual style the elements were not unfamiliar. A blue-and-gold style had been familiar since the Chinese T'ang era and was used by late Ming artists for their more mellifluous works. The Ming dynasty itself was a period of architectural grandiloquence when artists were expected to match the grandiose architecture with decorations of equal stature. But in painting (as opposed to craftwork) the Chinese never solved the problem of how to use their delicate implements on the grand scale, whereas the Japanese did so with tremendous energy and panache. Yashiro thinks that 'there must have been some decisive influence from Spanish Baroque art' but it is very difficult to imagine that the Japanese could have seen any Western Baroque on the grand scale. The elements of the new style were indeed already assembled in Japan and only awaited the setting and encouragement to be liberated. The Japanese decorators awoke to the possibilities inherent in the scale they were asked to exploit. The confidence of these artists is often startling and quite rivalled that of their masters. The snobbism that demanded slavish imitation of things Chinese was swept away. The *recherché* atmosphere of Ashikaga faded out before the swagger of Nobunaga and his successors.

Occasionally an artist was gifted enough to preserve something of Chinese taste and give it new meaning in a modern Japanese context. Such was Hasegawa Tōhaku (1539–1610). He admired Sesshū and even fought a court case to establish his right to style himself 'Sesshū the Fifth'. In the plate on page 141 Tōhaku makes a screen from pine-trees in the morning mist. The soft landscape is essentially Japanese. In his love of his native land he is the true successor of Sesshū. The soft brown ink fading into the paper, the reliance on tonality and atmosphere, the simplicity of the composition have all the elements of drama. Tōhaku's genius lies in his ability to enlarge such a scene without loss of sensibility and without the composition faling apart, leaving large areas of plain vacuity. The Japanese, with their concentration on technique, often push a means to the extreme without knowing where to stop. Tōhaku succeeds through the lyrical quality of his vision. The subject would not seem to lend

Tōhaku

PLATE P. 141

177

itself to the grandeur and brilliance which the atmosphere of the time demanded, but Tōhaku appeals to the romantic longing for simplicity and harmony in the Japanese temperament. He had learned from Chinese painting how to represent the nobility and statuesque quality of pine-trees, so important in all Far Eastern painting, and give them an atmosphere of cool, mist-shrouded elegance and strength. He had also learned from Chinese painting how to leave out unnecessary details. Each screen is skilfully varied; the trees have an almost human presence. No gaudy colours distract the eye; no complicated intertwinings flatter the senses. The austerity is softened, the pretentious rejected. Here once again empty spaces have the significance which they do in the best Sung Chinese masterpieces of landscape, with their elusive quality of unspoken solitude. Nothing could be further from the improvement on nature of Eitoku. The robustness associated with Momoyama art is totally absent. Tōhaku's power to evoke and reflect the mood of a cool early morning before sun and wind disperse the mists make this painting one of the most haunting of all landscapes.

Christianity Hitherto, the story of Japanese art has been much concerned with the Buddhist faith. Yet another of the world's great religions had to reach Japan — Christianity. However, its success, though great at first, was to be short-lived. It reached Japan through Portuguese Jesuit missionaries — notably Francis Xavier in the middle of the sixteenth century at the very end of the Ashikaga period. The early missionaries were well received and the future looked promising. When Nobunaga came to power a number of military men and simple people adopted the faith. Nobunaga met one of the early missionaries and seemed well disposed towards him — possibly because he disliked the Buddhists whose political ambitions had given him such trouble. Thus during his reign of thirteen years he supported and protected the Christians. Churches were built and the number of the faithful increased quite rapidly, a success which owed much to the decadence of most of the Buddhist sects of the time. A number of important lords adopted the faith and showed themselves sincere in their convictions. The Japanese, always curious about foreign customs, began to wear European decorative objects, and

European Christian motifs began to find their way into the arts, even on the armour of the warriors.

Of course, the most far-reaching Western innovation which the Portuguese brought with them was firearms. In a country quick to appreciate the value of a weapon which gave such an advantage they were soon adopted and led to the destruction of many fort-resses of the time which were defenceless against them.

The most interesting effect left by the Portuguese strangers on Japa-nese art can be seen in a series of screens called Namban or 'Southern Barbarian' screens which show the dress and behaviour of the foreigners. The format is completely Japanese but the figures are European and tellingly portrayed. The Japanese artists seem to have enjoyed the opportunity for portraiture presented by the strong features and strange dress of the missionaries. Though Western habits often disgusted them, they enjoyed painting genre scenes of Portuguese life in Japan; their ability to bring out the atmosphere of the settlements made their work highly sought after both inside Japan and in far-off Portugal, whither they were taken by Portu -guese ships. *'Southern Barbarian' screens*

PLATE P. 160

We know nothing of the artists who painted these screens; some of them may have received their training in Christian seminaries. Some of the paintings which are quite closely inspired by Western originals, of which a few exist, probably came from Western illustrated books. However, after only fifty years the wind of persecution began to blow and the influence of Western Christian art was abruptly cut short (see Chapter IX).

There is one sphere of art we have not hitherto touched on in this book: textiles and costume. From earliest times the Japanese have been fascinated by materials and their decoration — perhaps far more so than the Chinese. Naturally, following the cultural domi-nance of China, Chinese styles were at times popular, especially from the sixth to the eighth centuries, but in Japan upper-class dress has always presented more opportunities for variety and change of fashion than in China, where court fashion, for instance, seems to have been fairly slow to change and very circumscribed by etiquette. The twelve-layered dress of the ladies at the Fujiwara court must TEXTILES AND COSTUME have been breathtaking. The Japanese explored very many methods of decorating textiles — not only embroidery and brocades but dyeing by a number of methods, painting, applied gold leaf or gold dust on wet lacquer and then in combinations of various techniques to give variety.

Textile design However, it is not so much the techniques which give Japanese textiles their originality as their approach to design. The Japanese dress or kimono is fundamentally very simple in cut and has changed little. The effect comes from the design itself. The textile designers often looked on a robe as a total area to be decorated rather than as a piece of material which they then intended to make up into a robe. The total effect was uppermost in their minds — especially when designing robes for stage performances. It was part of Hideyoshi's plan to encourage the arts and crafts and he brought back and settled in the Nishijin area of Kyōtō weavers who had fled in earlier times. Nishijin has kept its foremost place in the silk-weaving industry ever since.

The styles of Momoyama were a blend of many elements — Ming grandiose style incorporating rich materials or precious metals, Muromachi refinement, even European and Indian textiles. The most powerful impulse came from the Kanō painted screens with their bold areas of gold and colour and the strong lines of painting. In fact, the designers of robes seem to have treated their textiles as a European painter would a canvas.

As with the screens, one is immediately impressed with the sense of daring and unconventionality in all these designs. The genius of the Japanese lies in their ability to harmonize what would at first appear to be impossible designs or colours. A robe divided into two parts vertically would in the West belong to a clown. In Japan it is a masterpiece of design, overwhelming in its resplendence, dignity and originality. It is an art of contrasts — colour and plain, crowded and sparse, shining and dull, light and dark, delicate and bold, geometrical and natural forms, simple and complicated.

PLATE P. 159 The robe in the plate on page 159 belonged to Tokugawa Ieyasu, for it bears his *mon* or crest on the shoulders; he gave it to a troupe of Nō actors. The colours are an unusual combination of geometrical and natural forms and the asymmetry of the design together with the richness of the material itself must have created a dazzling effect in the lights of the stage. One must remember that everything about the action of Japanese stage performances is strong and impressive. The actors needed powerful robes to match. The dyeing of material reached great heights. One particular technique requires mention: the *tsuji-ga-hana* method by which the colour was tie-dyed by stitching and the outlines added in ink. The actual family crests were in themselves most decorative and were used to great effect from this time onwards. Even used boldly and alone they are a most satisfying design. From the Momoyama period onwards the concept of the unity of all the arts is reinforced by textiles, for eminent artists would devote themselves to the design of robes. Each robe was an original creation by an artist and not an oft-repeated craft work. The balance of forms and colours is very modern to Western eyes. A robe such as this is a showpiece intended to raise its wearer out of the humdrum world of reality. If the screen-painter was allowed to gild the lily, how much more would the dressmaker be encouraged to adorn the human figure. This is not the restrained

FIGS. 57 to 59 – *Family crests (mon) of Nobunaga, Hideyoshi and Ieyasu. Cf. above.*

taste which we associate with Japan but the opposite extreme which one must accept in the Japanese spirit, as a violent outburst after restraint.

POTTERY   With the Momoyama period Japanese ceramics begin to demand serious consideration. They are quite unlike the accomplished, technically perfect Chinese wares and have to be appreciated on a different level. They are far more like the craft works of modern potters with which we in the West are familiar. Indeed many modern Western potters have learned much from them. Together with the Sung Chinese wares they provide the two main sources of Western ceramic inspiration. The popularity of the tea ceremony created a large market for the craft potters, who quickly became individual masters admired for their originality and for the expression of their personality in clay — Picasso in one period of his life presents an obvious parallel. In their expression of personality, they differ from the thousands of humble unnamed Chinese craftsmen working with amazing technical precision in the great factories of China.

One of the few results of Hideyoshi's Korean campaigns was that he brought back as prisoners Korean potters who pursued their craft in Japan. Their influence was particularly strong in the south

Karatsu ware   of Kyūshū Island, where Karatsu ware was produced for about three hundred years from approximately 1600, and in almost as

PLATE P. 162   many kilns. The products are strong and utilitarian, unlike those intended for the tea ceremony, but on these everyday objects the potters often .painted in iron oxide designs of great freedom and vigour, recalling the *tz'u-chou* ware of Sung China. Pottery in the style of the Korean Yi dynasty (1392–1910) began to influence the old Seto kilns, which in the late sixteenth century for a time moved to the nearby Mino prefecture. Here they made 'yellow Seto', Shino and Oribe wares. The first of these had a yellow opaque glaze over

Shino ware   an incised decoration of brown or green. Shino products usually have a thick white glaze over a brown decoration; a particularly attractive grey Shino has a white paste covered with grey-brown glaze with an incised decoration which reveals the white paste, after which the whole is covered with white glaze. The designs in both

釣便

不簑不笠不乘舠
日坐東軒學釣鼇
常載酒徐俟香餌出
輕鰌

賓欹相遇

PLATE 52 – Album-leaf 'The Convenience of Fishing' by Ike-no-Taiga (1723–76). Ink and soft colours on paper. *17.8 × 17.8 cm. Y. Kawabata Collection, Kamakura. Cf. p. 200.*

PLATE 53 – A pair of screens, 'Pine-trees in the Snow' by Maruyama Ōkyō (1733–95). Ink,

colours and gold dust on paper. *Each screen 155 × 335 cm. T. Mitsui Collection, Tokyo. Cf. p. 201.*

PLATE 54 – Album-leaf 'Autumn Landscape' by Gyokudō (1745–1820). *28.9 × 22.2 cm. H. Umezawa Collection, Tokyo. Cf. p. 200.*

PLATE 55 – 'Lovers Seated on a Balcony.' Wood-block print in *chūban* format by Suzuki Harunobu (1725–70), *c.* 1766–7. *National Museum, Tokyo. Cf. p. 213.*

PLATE 56 – Kansei-bijin ('Three Beauties of the Kansei Era'). Wood-block print by Kitagawa Utamarō (1753/4–1806), *c.* 1792–3. *Private Collection. Cf. p. 213.*

PLATE 57 – 'The Actor Segawa Kikunojō III as Ishizu in the play *Hana-a-yame Bunroku-sōga*', by Tōshūsai Sharaku (active 1794–5). *Private Collection. Cf. p. 214.*

PLATE 58—Detail from one of a pair of screens, "Eight Views of the Hsiao and Hsiang Rivers" by the Kano Master Naonobu (1607-50).

types have an individual freedom which recalls the dashing designs of Sung *tz'u-chou* types.

A very individual type is the Oribe ware, called after a late sixteenth-century tea-master, Furuta Oribe. In the green Oribe type a deep green glaze predominates, and the designs tend to be stylized landscapes worked out in geometric forms which tie in with the designs on fabrics. Some even have Christian motifs in their decoration. *Oribe ware*

Perhaps the best known are the *raku* wares from a kiln which is said to have been founded by one of the most illustrious figures in the history of Japanese ceramics, Chōjiro (1515–92). He was guided by the most famous of the early tea-masters, Sen-no-Rikyū. The word *raku* or 'pleasure' comes from a seal with this character on it which Hideyoshi is said to have given to Chōjiro's son, Tōkei. It was used to sign the pieces, and variations of this seal have been used by fourteen generations of *raku*-ware potters in the family down to the present day. The ware, usually simple tea-bowls, is low-fired on a small foot with a black, salmon-coloured or white glaze. Occasionally the colours are used to form a simple decoration. *Raku ware*
PLATE P. 163

It is difficult to explain the attraction of these bowls with their irregular shapes and rough glazes. They are the essence of tea-ceremony taste. Their shapes nestle in the hand and communicate the energy and personality of their makers. They seem to have a life of their own. The green tea in the bottom of the bowls as one drinks vividly sets off the colours. They are simple yet highly cultivated and have the quality of being able to harmonize with whatever else is assembled at the ceremony: a piece of rich brocade or an iron kettle, a whisk of bamboo or a piece of *tatami* matting. They look sturdy, yet this impression is false. Above all, these tea-ceremony wares have a sculptural quality. Much nonsense is talked and written about Japanese tea-ceremony wares, and there is a cult of the antique and ugly which sometimes blinds one to the subtlety of such pieces; but to appreciate the tea ceremony and the taste it stimulated one must understand *raku* ware.

The short Momoyama period was a prelude to the long Tokugawa era which followed and in many respects it is reasonable to consider the two together. By the time that Tokugawa Ieyasu died in 1616 the foundation had been laid for nearly two and a half centuries of prosperity and peace. After the battle of Sekigahara in 1600 the Tokugawa plans became clear. The new rulers were determined to increase their military strength to an absolute, unchallengeable level. This involved stripping the most powerful lords of their wealth, which they did with such success that they rapidly amassed control of a quarter of the national income. This increase in their personal wealth was made easier by the development of a national economy stimulated by peace and controlled on a national level. In 1601 the Tokugawa began to mint gold and silver coins which further filled their treasury, although later it became clear that they did not understand the problems and dangers of modern currency and its manipulation. The centres of trade were securely under the control of Tokugawa officials and, despite the rapacity of some of these appointees, the net gain in wealth was enormous. They even encouraged foreign trade in the early years until they began to see the missionaries as a potential military threat.

An indispensable adjunct of the Tokugawa plan was to destroy any possible internal threat, whether from the throne, feudal barons, peasants, artisans or traders. By the famous thirteen 'Rules for Military Houses' of 1615 they exacted unconditional obedience from the *daimyōs*, the 'Great Lords'. This recipe with its emphasis on the study of literature and the practice of military arts, frugality, obedience and sacrifice has a Chinese Confucian flavour. After the battle of Ōsaka in 1615, in which the supporters of Hideyoshi's descendants were wiped out, the process of levelling the greatest lords was speeded up. The fiefs were redistributed with strategic ends in view. Some areas of the greatest importance were placed under the control of the most trusted families, the 'Inner Lords', while the other areas under the 'Outer Lords', who were less well trusted, were rendered harmless. All were kept under constant surveillance; a system was developed whereby they were required to attend personally in the new capital of Edo (the present-day Tokyo) or to leave hostages there. The very expense in which they were thereby involved helped to deprive them of the means of sedition. Their castles were reduced in numbers and building was closely controlled. Communications were improved and closely supervised. The throne lost even more power but at the same time was supported economically. It was left for ceremonial functions only, but was able to survive two hundred and fifty years of humiliation to rise again in 1868.

The court nobles became less significant than the smallest feudal lords. As well as a highly efficient army the Tokugawa surrounded themselves with faithful and efficient, if sometimes rapacious, administrators. Ieyasu's personal reputation stood very high. He *Ieyasu* emerges as a ruthless and cruel man but it can be argued that, in his age, the conditions and the need to succeed forced him to be so. Both militarily and politically he was a good strategist, prepared to make long-term plans and work with single-mindedness towards the achievement of his ends. He himself lived up to the high Confucian moral code and was frugal even to the extent of miserliness. Building on the work of Nobunaga and Hideyoshi, he was able to use his strength of will and sound judgement to ensure the continuation of his line. An admirer of Yoritomo and a man of intense personal courage, he had a cold and ruthless streak in his character which does not endear him to history.

One of his greatest problems was the large number of unemployed *Social problems* samurai now at large in a country that had settled down to peace. The *rōnin* or 'wave men', as they were called, estimated at as many as half a million, were often unemployable and formed a constant source of social and political mischief. Most of them were denied the opportunity of using any talents they might have developed in administration, for example, and they created centres of potential subversion.

The peasantry as usual were harshly burdened but, instead of fleeing to less populated areas, they now swelled to excess the population of the bustling capital and larger towns. Both they and the merchants shared in the development of new wealth and served the families that were forced to live under surveillance in Edo. The merchants in particular enriched themselves and eventually emerged as the most powerful class. Edo expanded rapidly, as did other towns which served as commercial centres. Class barriers tended to crumble beneath the impact of the new wealth.

Drive against Christianity At the beginning of the period the wind seemed set fair for a rapid expansion of international trade, but the Tokugawa rulers soon began to fear the influence of foreign missionaries. They were well informed about the activities of the missionaries in China and the Philippines and, like the Chinese emperors of the eighteenth century, they found the quarrels between Jesuits and Franciscans distasteful. The possibility of discontented feudal lords allying themselves with foreign powers was a very obvious threat. The anti-Christian orders of 1611–4 were followed by more drastic decrees in 1633, 1634 and 1639, particularly after a rising at Shimabara in 1637–8 which seemed to be inspired by vague Christian ideals. Here some 37,000 simple people were driven to revolt by economic hardship but only about one hundred escaped the Tokugawa wrath. Christianity was then strictly prohibited and the isolation laws *Isolation policy* tightened up. Summary execution awaited any Japanese who tried to leave the country or to return after more than five years' absence. From 1641 onwards only a few Chinese and a handful of Dutch were allowed to live in a very closely circumscribed settlement on Deshima Island near Nagasaki. The Tokugawa felt that it would be safe to let them stay there in order to pass on medical knowledge which they thought would be harmless. The martyrdom of the Japanese Christians furnished some of the blackest pages in religious persecution — and this at the hands of a people until then singularly tolerant in religious matters.

In this atmosphere of seclusion Japan shut itself in a hothouse where its culture was forced and inbred. The wealth and energies of a vigorous, expanding people were spent in pleasure and rich living. The Japanese were denied the satisfactions of intellectual experiment which the West enjoyed from the seventeenth century onwards and their efforts seemed to be expended at feverish pace in pleasure and the arts. The new merchant class grew in power and wealth. Even the economic crises and devaluations of currency seem to have left them richer. Thus a process which started in the Ashikaga period continued further until the merchants ended by becoming the arbiters of taste, patrons of the most lively arts and the real holders of power. Despite strenuous efforts the Tokugawa failed to curb their outward show of this wealth. Edo in particular became a city where quick fortunes could be made and spent; its working men became notorious for their gullibility and spendthrift ways. The hordes of travellers coming to the city to indulge themselves brought new riches to shopkeepers and those who served them. Edo soon gained a reputation as a boisterous, lawless city of pleasure.

In art the tendencies of the Momoyama period were amply fulfilled. A distinctive school of decorative painting flowered in the Edo period which owes its foundation to the genius of Sōtatsu. His predecessor, the calligrapher and arbiter of taste Kōetsu (1558–1632), had founded an artistic community at Takagamine in the outskirts of Kyōtō, which served as a centre of singularly modern type where craftsmen and painters could influence one another's works. Here Sōtatsu mixed with men of talent and taste. Occasionally Kōetsu did the calligraphy for paintings by Sōtatsu, a combination of effort which one finds in both China and Japan.

PAINTING

Sōtatsu

We know little about the life of Sōtatsu. He may have come from a family of textile dealers or fan-makers and was active from about 1596 to 1623. His style owed its origins to decorative paintings of the Tosa school which had so successfully illustrated tales from literature and history. Sōtatsu sought inspiration from the same source but treated this only as a stepping-off point for an original decorative treatment. The essence of his style is the bold use of sweeping areas of colour, for which ink also served, in seemingly simple compositions of nostalgic charm and unerringly effective spacing. His work is the epitome of one side of Japanese taste. For this the rhythms must be carefully controlled, the vigour of execution and sensitivity of conception carefully balanced, and colour used unobtrusively to create a mood. Variations on a theme are worked out as in a play, often creating the effect of a tableau enacted against a sweeping background of colour laid on with a huge brush.

PLATE P. 164 One of his most notable achievements is the Sekiya screen, which depicts an incident in the famous *Tale of Genji* by the eleventh-century woman novelist Lady Murasaki. According to a passage in the novel, early in his career Prince Genji encountered the Lady Utsusemi but their romance did not prosper. She subsequently married a provincial governor and went to live in a distant province. In this scene the governor, after a visit to Kyōtō, was taking Utsusemi back via the famous Ōsaka frontier hill. Genji, who had now returned from exile, was by chance attending a service at the nearby Ishiyama shrine; recognizing who was in the carriage, he said jestingly to her brother that it was not often that he showed such attentiveness by travelling to the barrier to meet anybody. When Utsusemi heard this she was deeply touched by old memories. The story has the ingredient of hopeless love which always moves the Japanese. The composition is reduced to its essentials, the colours simplified and the diagonals carefully balanced. The background is like a setting for a stage play, carefully contrived to suggest a time and place and to evoke an atmosphere. In a peculiarly effective way all attention is focussed on the closed carriage where an unseen lady sits, her heart beating, afraid to look at her former love playing a gallant little role outside, half serious and half in jest. One senses that the few retainers appreciate the situation and are a little perturbed by the implications of this unexpected meeting. In this tableau the ox alone has a sense of movement and presses forward as if threatening Genji; it is an element of power and action between the two static bodies of carriage and prince. Very cleverly Sōtatsu has made the animal the link between the two, thereby furnishing the one element of dynamism the composition requires. In this one decorative scene many elements of Japanese taste and sensibility combined. It is as conventionalized as much of Japanese life and as restrained as one aspect of its social mores. Most important, the barrier at the pass symbolizes the obstacles between the two former lovers and subtly suggests the dangers involved in passing it.

One needed, of course, a knowledge of literature to enjoy such a picture to the full. To understand much of Japanese art one must appreciate the understatement and the subtlety of suggestion, the restraint and the formality which hedge human relations.

The decorative tendencies of the Edo period stimulated by Sōtatsu and his school bore fruit fifty years later and are summarized in the art of the period 1680–1730/40, generally known by the name of a period within it as the Genroku period (1688–1703). These years *Genroku period* saw the emergence of a number of notable artists in various fields who worked in an atmosphere of wealth adequate to support their activities and to enable them to enjoy their visual pleasures. Moronobu and Kiyonobu, the print artists (see below) were also working at this time. Ninsei and Kenzan were active in ceramics, and the brilliant *yūzen* printed textile technique reached its highest peak of development. Without doubt Ōgata Kōrin (1658–1716) was the spokesman of the *Kōrin* age. He was born in 1658, in a family which ran a textile shop, whence he obtained a lively acquaintance with design. His family was wealthy and professionally well connected both with the noble ruling class and by marriage with the Hon'ami family, to which belonged Sōtatsu and Kōetsu, whom we mentioned above. They supplied members of the Tokugawa shōgunate with robes and were sufficiently prosperous to count themselves among the ranks of the merchant class who rose in society by lending money to impoverished *daimyōs*. The father of Kōrin and his brother, the potter Kenzan, had inherited the family dress concern Karigane-ya. He was himself a calligrapher and painter in a style which combined the Kanō and Tosa styles. He was keen on the theatre and obviously more interested in the arts than in business. He gave Kōrin ample money to devote himself to a life of pleasure and enjoyment of the arts and society. This, together with the accumulated debts of the store, brought him into financial difficulties, so that by about 1696 he was forced to take up a career as designer of kimono; Kenzan, in equal difficulties, built a kiln and set up as a manufacturer of ceramics, a craft he had studied under Ninsei. Kōrin drew the designs for *FIG. 63* many of his products. Thus financial difficulties forced the two talented brothers to embark upon an artistic career. Kōrin worked mostly in Kyōtō but for a time (1704–9) tried his fortune in Edo. However, he was not happy there and returned to Kyōtō, where he ended his life in poverty but very active.

Without doubt the greatest influence on Kōrin's artistic development was the work of Sōtatsu, whose compositions he often reinterpreted. He had studied the various other schools — Kanō, the genre work of Itchō, and even the forerunners of the colour-print movement. Elements of all these diverse stylistic tendencies are found in the products of this versatile and talented artist. But most critics regard as his masterpiece, and as representative of his mature
PLATE P. 165 work, the famous pair of screens 'Red and White Plum-trees' in the Atami Museum. In this bold combination of art and nature, gnarled trees put out their spring flowers against a brilliant background of gold. A swollen stream, swirling in rhythmic curves, is splashed in a solid area of dark colour down the centre of the composition and dominates it in a manner which some Japanese feel to be almost sinister. Much of the power of the design lies in the relative naturalism of the trees compared with the flat, vertical and unnaturalistic stream. The design of the trees themselves is strikingly opposed; unlike many decorative works, the painting has an inner tension which gives it unusual power and intensity. It is pure decoration in that, apart from the symbolism of plum-trees for spring-time, it requires no knowledge of literature but only abandonment to the rich visual effect of design and colour.

Chinese influence Despite the dynamic new streams of purely Japanese art in the Tokugawa period, and the efforts of the new rulers to exclude foreign influences, Chinese artists continued to make themselves felt. The type of Chinese painting popular at this time is known in China as *wên-jên* painting. It was an art of scholars or cultivated men who were supposed to pursue painting as a spare-time occupation, a means whereby they could express their most lofty spiritual aspirations. This amateur tradition of painting in China was extremely ancient, having originated in the late T'ang dynasty in approximately the eighth and ninth centuries. The style was known in
Bun-jin painting Japan as *bun-jin* painting, from the Japanese reading of the characters *wên-jên*. In China it became involved with what is known as

'Southern painting', the style developed by artists who lived in the misty atmospheric world of South China and whose brushwork was abbreviated. By the seventeenth and eighteenth centuries these trends had coalesced into two main streams. The first was that of the more conservative scholars who painted in a meticulous style based on the great masters of the past, especially of the Ming dynasty. Their work, often large landscapes filling the whole 'canvas', is highly detailed and has strong literary overtones. The second stream was that of a group of individualists who, though claiming an equally ancient heritage, deliberately tried to escape from the heavy weight of tradition and produce something entirely new within the tradition. Both streams of painting entered Japan and were taken up by Japanese painters with enthusiasm.

The *bun-jin* movement in Japan started about 1700 and was firmly established about half a century later. Its first great exponents were *Buson* Yōsa Buson (1716–83) and Ike-no-Taiga (1723–76). Buson is equally known as a poet and in fact abandoned painting to devote his last years in Kyōto to literature. The plate on page 166, a land- PLATE P. 166; scape painted on a sliding door, shows strong elements of Chinese Sung and Ming dynasty brushwork in the rocks and trees, allied with the typical southern mood of mists and intimate communion with nature. However, the whole workmanship is infused with the nervous energy of the Japanese brush. As with much Japanese painting of the time it is somewhat eclectic, taking elements from various Chinese sources of the Ming and Ch'ing dynasties; a detailed study would reveal many different sources, which in China might even conflict. The whole approach is more on the surface than in a Chinese painting, with a strong appeal to immediate visual effects and a seeming unwillingness to proceed deeper. It thus tends to be a little synthetic and dry, but nevertheless as a decoration in Chinese style it is the work of a sensitive master. Taiga shows in his large and small works more of the free impressionistic brushwork which is associated with 'Southern painting'. The plate on page 183 is from one of his best-known albums, 'The Ten Conveniences and the Ten Enjoyments of Country Living', of which Taiga did the Conveniences and Buson the Enjoyments — all inspired by poems written by Li Li-wêng, a Chinese poet of the last dynasty. This 'Convenience of Fishing' has soft colours and bold amusing lines which evoke the rustic atmosphere. The paintings extol the carefree other-worldliness of the Nanga or Southern painters and are the outcome of a semi-serious longing for the simple pleasures of country living, far removed from the commitments of a sophisticated way of life. It is second-hand in that it is the Chinese scholar's dream taken over by a Japanese. The landscapes are more intimate than their Chinese counterparts and the basic Japanese tendency to reduce a scene to rhythmic formulae is often visible.

Gyokudō The tendency towards a freer interpretation of landscape and a more Japanese style of brushwork is seen at its best in the work of Gyokudō (1745–1820). Gyokudō started in the service of a local lord and, when the latter died in 1798, travelled throughout Japan, finally settling in Kyōtō. He was well-known for his calligraphy and poetry, and was also an accomplished musician — in fact the ideal Chinese scholar-administrator such as those upon whom he modelled his life. The small landscape from an album in the plate on page 190 is typical of his work and takes the Chinese individualist painters of the eighteenth century one step further. The landscape is dissolved into a complicated skein of light lines and hasty colour washes. The mountains are humpy outlines and seemingly random russet washes suggest the foliage of autumn. His unmistakable style is a combination of lightness and wit, of powerful rhythms expressed in arbitrary but sensitive brushwork. By a simple use of line and colour he achieves a mood and an emotion which are unforced and make this an individual contribution to Far Eastern landscape painting. Most significant is the proof his work gives that, whereas the Chinese individualist inspiration seems to have run out in the last quarter of the eighteenth century, the Japanese were prepared to continue their experiments, impelled perhaps by the constant public demand for originality which activated almost all classes of society.

Western influence Although the Tokugawa rulers were obsessed with the desire to keep Japan isolated from the rest of the world, a considerable amount of information about the West did filter through to the starved intellectual circles of Japan. The main channel for this was the Dutch settlement at Nagasaki, where a few Chinese also lived; they were able to introduce a number of the innovations in the art of painting· which were being made in the fertile cultural climate of cities like Yangchou and Hangchou. One senses these innovations in the work of Taiga and Gyokudō.

The Japanese were naturally highly intrigued by the naturalism of Western art, about which they learned from engravings in Western scientific books and at second hand through Chinese artists. Truth to nature had never been a tradition of Eastern painting, in which abstraction and the achievement of the essence of a subject were all-important. Now elements of naturalism based on close observation of nature for a while became fashionable. The leading artist of this movement·was Maruyama Ōkyō (1733–95), who made the *Ōkyō* pilgrimage to Nagasaki to study the new mode. His most famous work, a pair of screens still owned by the Mitsui family which order- PLATE PP. 184-5 ed them, shows pine-trees in the snow. The snow lies heavily on the trunks and foliage in such a way that the impression is created of stillness and weight in the sunlit calm following the snow-fall. The work is the outcome of careful observation of nature. His other paintings show that he was equally a master of Kanō school ink work. In fact the more one looks at his products, the more one feels that he, too, is well in the tradition of Japanese painting. The brilliant gold background and the general dramatic treatment place him firmly in the ranks of the great decorators. Thus in a way it is proper to see some of Ōkyō's work as simply another aspect of the search for the striking in a sensation-seeking atmosphere. Countless stories are told of the accuracy of this painter's representations but none of his extant works show what we would consider an overwhelming degree of naturalism. However, his interpretations were sufficiently novel to appeal to an intellectually starved public vaguely conscious of changes taking place in the outside world. It is unlikely that pure truth to nature would have interested the Japanese any more than it did the Chinese.

It has always counted for much in the eyes of Eastern painters to be patronized by the ruling class. Court painters in China and Japan have been assured of good livings and honourable positions in society. The Tokugawa shōguns, like most Far Eastern rulers, encouraged literature and the arts; in painting they supported the *Kanō school* Kanō school, not only with commissions but with land, houses and patronage on a princely scale. The Kanō painters ranged from those who supplied the shōguns to those who painted for lesser ranks of the nobility and so on down the scale. The provincial lords, quick to follow their masters in Edo, provided work for many others. The painters in this school were legion and often their work shows the kind of monotony which comes from easy living and the need only to follow time-worn formulae. True, they were not assisted by the subjects which the Tokugawa rulers favoured — Confucian moralizing scenes which meant relatively little to the governing class of seventeenth-century Japan and nothing at all to the general public.

FIG. 60 – *'Lovers' by Hishikawa Moronobu. C. 1682. Hillier Collection. Cf. p. 212.*

In Chinese painting a stylistic innovation such as a way of painting rocks or trees rapidly became an accepted form which lasted for centuries. The Kanō masters used many of these old brush-stroke styles which give the impression of strength of brush (a quality always admired and one that presented no great technical difficulty to the Japanese) but often allied to shallow themes and artistic clichés. The impression is thus often one of insincerity and pose. It is easy to be over-critical of most Kanō works of this type, but we should perhaps judge them by a different standard from that applied to genuine creative works. They may not be quite so low down in the scale as commercial wall-paper designs but are roughly on a level with the Western chinoiserie which so captivated Europe in the eighteenth century. Although not animated by any desire to break new ground or see the world about with intense or fresh eyes, they are at least fine works of decoration which combine the breadth of scale of the great screen-painters with Japanese skill in brushwork. The Chinese brush is essentially an intimate tool and when the scale becomes inflated, as it did also in much Chinese Ming court painting, it often fails to carry the weight.

No greater gulf exists than that between the Kanō school and the *Colour-prints* work of the last great movement in painting we shall illustrate, that of the Japanese colour-print. It entails a leap as great as that from the routine and complacency of nineteenth century French Academy paintings to the revolutionary visions of van Gogh and Gauguin.

It is obviously impossible in a book of this scope to give a full appreciation of the colour-print, one of Japan's greatest contributions to the world's store of art. It was through this peculiar art form that the West came to know Japanese art at the end of the last century, although a peculiar snobbism had led to its underestimation by the intellectual classes of Japan itself. A recent book by an eminent Japanese authority can still ignore it, and it is largely owing to Western appreciation that it won the position of dignity it now enjoys.

The reasons for the rise of the colour-print, known in Japanese as *Origins* Ukiyo-e, or 'Paintings of the Floating (or Fleeting) World', are many and varied. Japanese painters as early as the Momoyama period

showed great interest in genre scenes, in the activities of their fellow men, their surroundings, pursuits and above all their dress. Even earlier the Kamakura scrolls, as we have seen, delighted in the human situation. The textiles of the Momoyama and early Edo periods above all were irresistible in design. Even Kanō school painters, trained in the most rigid classical manner, could not resist genre scenes, although they never signed such work. In early genre paintings, for example in the painting of bath-house girls who were little more than prostitutes, one can already see both an awareness of the value to painting of everyday subjects and the expression of a sense of humour quite alien to the Chinese approach. A fresh wind is blowing through art.

Ukiyo-e was an art intended to serve a new society in Japan — 'the prosperous, creative and illegitimate élite of shopkeepers and entertainers at the bottom of the Japanese social order' — to whom the heavily charged Chinese-style Kanō paintings meant little. These chōnin or townspeople, especially in the upstart nouveau riche capital of Edo, were very little interested in Confucian moralizing themes, whereas the colourful world around them provided an endless source of spontaneous inspiration which found reflection in a large output of literature and art. Once Japan had been closed to all outside contacts and the country became increasingly prosperous, frankly emphasizing luxury and easy living, the people who spent their money so freely were also determined to have paintings about them which reflected this life and titivated their imagination. As the population of the towns grew, so the lower classes began to share in the prosperity and sought paintings to decorate their houses. To meet their needs a cheap method of reproduction by means of wood-block printing was developed, which reached tremendous proportions. The essence of the Ukiyo-e atmosphere has been summed up by Hibbett as 'an unreflective enjoyment of the moment — a moment valued for present pleasure, but to be savoured with discrimination'.

Fig. 61 – 'Woman Looking over her Shoulder', by Kaigetsudō Anchi. C. 1715. Art Institute of Chicago. Cf. p. 211.

Dashing and irreverent, it opened up a completely new world of inexhaustible delight.

Chinese influence The technique itself was not new. In the T'ang dynasty Chinese Buddhists had made popular iconographic representations by means of wood block-printing and in the Heian period Japanese devotees printed in colour on fans, which were then written over with the holy *sūtras*. The Chinese in the seventeenth century made the famous books of woodcuts known as the *Mustard Seed Garden* and the *Ten Bamboo Studio*, as well as a number of popular erotic pictures in the medium, and it was certainly these which gave the Japanese the inspiration for their movement. However, as so often happened, the Japanese took a Chinese invention and developed it to a degree undreamed of by the Chinese. They made it the most sophisticated, prolific art ever produced for the plebeian classes in any civilization. This was an inexpensive form of art available for a few pennies to everyone. It mirrored the world about them, illustrated their stories old and new, lionized their actors, flattered their courtesans. In these colour-prints the changing parade of fashion passes before our eyes; we are taken through the landscape of Japan on journeys made dramatic in the most artistic manner; we spy on lovers, decent and indecent, and make fun of aristocrats caught in the most impossible amorous entanglements. Japan's great historical events are re-lived with bravura, poems and plays illustrated, festivities recorded. No art ever brought to life in such detail the world of its creators nor mirrored more faithfully the life of pleasure, with its undertones of sadness, typical of Japanese thought. Its prolificacy, complexity and quality dazzle the student.

Although this was a mass medium, it demanded many talents — as many as are involved in modern advertising, but in the Japanese case with more lasting artistic results. First, the man who commissioned the prints was an impresario in his own right, who was not only sensitive to fashion and the public taste but could also greatly influence the prints he asked his artists to design. The famous masters of the print movement now so familiar to us made their designs only to have them destroyed by the craftsmen, the skilled carvers who created the blocks; finally, there were the printers who

PLATE 59 – 'Mount Fuji Seen from Kanagawa.' From 'Thirty-six Views of Mount Fuji' by Katsushika Hokusai (1760–1849). *Cf. p. 215.*

PLATE 60 – Sword-guards and netsuke. *Ashmolean Museum, Oxford. Cf. p. 218f.*

PLATE 61 – (*Above left*). Old Kutani ware shallow dish. *Height 8.6 cm, diameter 41.2 cm. (Above right).* Kakiemon ware bowl with design of flowers and birds. *Height 21.1 cm, diameter 30.7 cm. M. Shiobara Collection, Tokyo. (Below left).* Large jar by Nonomura Ninsei. *Height 27.7 cm. Seikadō Foundation, Tokyo. (Below right).* Nabeshima ware vase with flowers, fruit and animals. *Height 30.6 cm. Private* ▶ *Collection. Cf. p. 220f.*

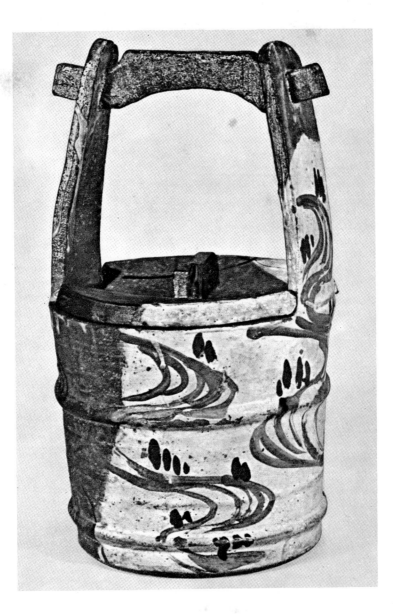

PLATE 62 – Water-container. Ceramic in the form of a wooden bucket with design of waves and marine plants on a white ground. Atelier of Kenzan. *Cf. p. 221.*

inked them with delicate skill and made the various blocks fit the registers with amazing accuracy. Of the innumerable thousands of prints, remarkably few produced before 1850 can be faulted for careless craftsmanship or feeble inspiration. The urban population faithfully supported their artists while the demand for originality drove them to ever more striking efforts.

The origin of the Ukiyo-e style is attributed to an almost legendary *Matabei* artist named Matabei (or Matahei) who lived in the mid-seventeenth century; he is said to have combined the colouring of Tosa school work with the powerful line of the Kanō school and applied the result to genre scenes. However, the man who popularized the style was Moronobu (1618 or 1625–95), who used wood block- *Moronobu* printing to illustrate books, of which he produced more than a hundred from 1672 onwards, and later for single-sheet prints. FIG. 60 Moronobu's women are short and plump, hardly distinguishable one from the other. Their robes are bold and simple, and show the interest which one would expect from the son of an embroiderer; the poses and composition are effective, embracing all the basic elements of Ukiyo-e art. The scenes have a rustic quality and suggest an unaffected enjoyment on the artist's part of the simple world about him. With Kaigetsudō the somewhat sketchy figures of Moro- *Kaigetsudō* nobu become full female figures of stature and power. From then on the female figure is one of the most dominant subjects. Kaigetsudō is a problem in that there are four men who sign themselves by this name. Japanese historians attribute these works to Andō, the founder of the 'school', and his three pupils, Anchi, Dōhan and Dōshin; some Europeans, on the other hand, think they were done by the same man who used different signatures. However this may be, they are all so similar in style as to merit their being treated as the work of one master. Andō painted beauties of Edo from 1704 to 1716; according to some authorities, he only painted and did not design prints. Kaigetsudō prints usually represent monumental figures in splendid robes massively outlined and coloured by hand in tan, buff, yellow and lilac colours. Everything about the print reproduced here, signed Kaigetsudō Anchi, has monumentality, FIG. 61 from the scale of the figure to the sweep of the dress with its figure of a poet and fragments of poetry in cursive script.[1] The rhythms are broad, the decorations powerful and even the features — outlined in a single line from hair to neck — are strong. This type of design had an influence on the female subjects which almost every subsequent artist attempted: women of the tea-houses and gay quarters in all their finery, and at every moment in their lives; famous women from history and literature; male actors in female roles; and, above all, the favourite courtesans of the pleasure quarters of Edo where, in a steamy, heady atmosphere, the pleasure-seekers dissipated their money and their energies. Here the most gracious prostitutes the world has known created a subtle, sophisticated world in which they practised their trade with the help of every possible refinement and artifice. Dressed in magnificent robes, attended by personal servants, they were treated like queens, pampered and spoiled for the brief moments of their ascendancy. It is no wonder that this colourful pageant absorbed the popular artists. As with the pin-up girls of our generation, their portraits found a ready market even among people who could not afford their company.

Of the many print-masters who contributed to the movement it is possible here to look at a few representative works by some of the greatest. Suzuki Harunobu (1725–70) is credited with the invention of *nishiki-e*, 'brocade painting' which involved printing with up to ten different colours faultlessly accurate in their register. Before him prints had been in black outline only and then coloured by hand or subsequently by two-coloured prints in red and green. Harunobu's female figures are petite and realistically Japanese in physique. He placed them in settings which related them convincingly to the world they inhabited, sometimes with gentle charm and sometimes quite dramatically or humorously.

The greatest artist of women was Kitagawa Utamarō (1753–1806), who dominated the movement in the 1790s. We are told that he

Harunobu
PLATE P 187,

Utamarō
PLATE P. 188

---

[1] Helen C. Gunsaulus, *The Clarence Buckingham Collection of Japanese Prints* (Art Institute of Chicago 1955).

actually resided in the Yoshiwara or pleasure quarter of Edo, where life revolved around the favourite courtesans of the moment. Its colourful life provided him with endless inspiration. His women are frankly idealistic — tall, willowy, light-hearted creatures as far removed from the real Japanese physical type as models in *Vogue* are from Western women who dream vainly of attaining their languorous shapes. They are in fact fashion plates and portraits of low society *par excellence*. Around these beauties swarm the dandies and *roués* who were their admirers and customers. Utamarō achieves his effect by bold effortless lines of great strength and cleanliness. Nothing is allowed to detract from the grand sweep of the figure. The dresses are superb and the emphasis is placed firmly on the feminine. Yet even he sometimes tired of the endless parade of women to make fine prints of natural objects and to portray passions other than those of the flesh.

Most connoisseurs of the Japanese print give pride of place to a very enigmatic artist, Tōshūsai Sharaku, about whom we know *Sharaku* almost nothing. The biographies say no more than that he may have been an actor turned artist. During a few months in 1794 and 1795 he produced a number of prints of actors which must have been so biting in their characterization that the public would not accept them. As a result his publishers were forced to drop him. The plate PLATE P. 189, on page 206 illustrates the actor Segawa Kikunojō III as Ishizu in the play *Hana-a-yame Bunroku-sōga*, produced in 1794. He is, of course, a man playing a woman's role, as was the convention in the Kabuki theatre. The technical skill with which male actors assume female characteristics is one of the delights of the Japanese stage. But one can understand that this portrayal must have been too revealing for the star-struck audience of his day. It is difficult not to see in it the same sense of humour that inspires some of the early masks. Although these prints remained unsold in Sharaku's day, they now command by far the highest prices of all the print-masters' works. The first half of the nineteenth century was dominated by two great designers, Hokusai and Hiroshige. Katsushika Hokusai was born in *Hokusai* 1760 to a family of craftsmen. At fifteen he worked for an engraver and by the age of nineteen entered the studio of Shunshō, a designer popular for his theatrical prints. For the next seventy years he devoted himself with fanatic purpose to painting and print designing, producing during his long life at least thirty thousand drawings and illustrations for five hundred books. He was a restless eccentric, changing his name some thirty times and moving house no less than ninety-three times — on one occasion twice in a single day. In an unhappy turbulent life, abandoned by all except his daughter, his dedication to art was the only steadying force. To the very end of his days he remained feverishly active, begging for a few more years in which he might perfect his art.

PLATE P. 207 His period of greatest maturity was between 1823 and 1845. We represent this protean talent with a landscape, perhaps his most famous, for it was to this art that he made such a great contribution. After one hundred and fifty years the print movement needed a new impetus. Landscape, at once the oldest and most respected of Eastern themes, provided the fresh inspiration; it was the genius of Hokusai which made the 'cockney' of Edo enjoy his visions of the grandeur of nature at its most romantic and sublime. He was aided by the fact that between 1802 and 1822 many books had been produced which served to guide tourists in the new craze for travel — made easier by good roads and improved communications under the Tokugawa. The fact that landscapes could become so popular among the townspeople shows once again the deep-rooted love of the Japanese for their own country. In the work of Hokusai they found prints of actual scenery transformed by an imagination of genius.

The Chinese painter tends to be in love with the *idea* of landscape. Both Hokusai and Hiroshige gave the public landscape which, though skilfully interpreted, they could recognize and associate themselves with. This was not Chinese super-refinement but something simply larger than life. Hokusai reduced the world about him to bold and original designs without losing touch with his subject. His artistic extravagance was founded on the same earthy passion which lay at the root of the whole print movement. A warm humanity flows through everything he did. For him the world was a vast theatrical backdrop against which man and his emotions are seen in their true puny status. His humour, and there is much, is never malicious. Towards the end of his life he turned increasingly to classical subjects, which he derived from a deep knowledge of the literature and history of China and Japan. Our illustration shows the warm and joyous themes which run through his appreciation of Japanese landscape. His compositions, although striking, are rarely forced or twisted merely for the sake of effect. His sense of line and colour is impeccable. His volumes of 'Random Sketches' are an FIG. 62 inexhaustible mine of original designs in which every movement of man and the world he inhabits becomes a source for an original work of art. He is a daemonic figure of colossal invention.

Ichiryūsai Hiroshige (1797–1858), the younger contemporary of *Hiroshige* Hokusai, came to the fore from 1826 onwards with his 'Views of the Eastern Capital' (about 1826), the first 'Tōkaidō' set (1834), 'Fa- PLATE P. I mous Views of Kyōtō' (1834) and the 'Eight Views of Lake Biwa' (1835). His genius for landscape produced an endless flow of designs inspired by the countryside. In them man acts out a more gentle role than in Hokusai; it was easier for the man-in-the-street to associate himself with the emotions of Hiroshige's personae as they emerge from the mists of morning, brave storms of rain, or plod up snow-covered slopes. Hillier remarks that 'Our sympathies are won over not only by his artistry, but by the sense that, though essentially Japanese, he is in some indefinable way closer to us, in style and sentiment, than any of his forerunners...'[1]

His success was phenomenal in terms of sales but unfortunately the blocks were used so often that late impressions give little idea of the delicacy of line and colour of the first editions. He produced some 5,400 different print designs, many of which are run-of-the-mill — but among them one finds many bold unconventional compositions and a surprising number of masterpieces. Night scenes, snow scenes, wind scenes, landscape in mist or rain — he was above all the master of atmosphere and poetic mood. His approach is more humble than that of Hokusai, his work less original and daring, less powerful

[1] J. Hillier, *Japanese Masters of the Colour Print* (London 1954), p. 25.

FIG. 62 – 'Random Sketches' (Manga), by Hokusai. After 1814. Cf. p. 215.

in draughtsmanship, less concerned with the deeper problems of life, and far less involved. He enjoyed his world, his success. His comments on the human scene arouse a smile which, unlike that we get from Hokusai, has no more serious undertones. Michener attributes Hiroshige's success in Europe to a number of factors — that his output was so enormous that in any early shipment of prints to Europe some were sure to be by Hiroshige, that Western artists like Turner had prepared the way for such interpretations of natural phenomena, and to the fact that Hiroshige's imagery is very easy to understand.[1] Certainly the travellers shown in the plate on page 1, from the 'Fifty-three Stations of the Tōkaidō', the great highway PLATE P. 1 linking Edo and Kyōtō, are figures of human proportions with whom we can easily sympathize.

This was an art tailored to and pandering to a wide market which was both discriminating and fickle. A changed hair-style could ruin the fortunes of a print; almost overnight a school or artist could be as outmoded as last year's hem-line. But talented designers pressed hard on one another's heels ready to invent, plagiarize or do anything to capture the market. They were forced always to be on their mettle artistically, to seek novelty, to outdo their rivals — and for nearly three hundred years they succeeded.

When Japan was finally opened to the West from about 1868, these *Influence on West* prints came to Europe as wrappings and packing material. Impressionist painters like Manet and his friends found in them a completely new approach to problems of painting which helped them to free themselves from traditions they hated. The new compositions were full of unexpected unconventional views, new uses of line and flat areas of colour. Degas and van Gogh were particularly impressed by this art from the mysterious land on the other side of the world, so long closed to Western eyes.

It is interesting that modern Japanese artists should have returned to the tradition of the colour-prints and found in them a fertile source of inspiration — the skill of the chisel on wood once used

---

1 James A. Michener, *The Floating World* (New York 1954), pp. 213-26.

for sculpture seems born in them. They have been more successful in this medium than in any other international art form.

The most striking aspect of the proliferating crafts in the Edo period is the meticulous interest with which the Japanese searched every aspect of nature for motifs. It seems that no object, animate or inanimate, was too trivial to be turned into the theme of a minuscule object of true art. The innate taste and high standards of the craftsmen throughout these centuries have never been approached by any other nation. The fact that people had relatively little else on which to spend their new wealth may have contributed to the huge output. The constant demand for the original meant that craftsmen seldom repeated themselves. Two particular fields in which these forces operated most strongly were *tsuba* or sword-guards and such accoutrements of dress as *inrō* or medicine-boxes and the sash buttons known as *netsuke*.

The sword-guard (top left in the plate on page 208) is of well-forged iron coated with black magnetic oxide. It was made by the Kinai school, active in Echizen province from the seventeenth to nineteenth century, and possibly founded by an offshoot of the most famous school of armourers, the Myōchin, which started in the twelfth century. The Kinai school was eminent in *tsuba* manufacture from the sixteenth century onwards. This example was probably made about 1800 and belongs to one of the most popular groups. The pierced relief of five cranes is most cunningly arranged in a very clean design. It is a constant source of delight to see how the manufacturers of these guards were able to exploit this difficult shape, often turning it to artistic advantage. The guard gives the impression of still being utilitarian rather than purely decorative.

The example at the bottom right is of the Ōmori school, founded in the early eighteenth century; like many later guards, it has a quality of workmanship which makes it akin to jewellery. Such guards were often given as presents among lords and never saw a sword-blade. It has a relief of various autumn plants — chrysanthemum, aster, gentian, begonia among others — and is richly encrusted with gold and silver. This particularly fine example is signed by Terumasa, who worked from 1704 to 1772. The metal is a unique Japanese alloy of copper with a small addition of gold which was then pickled to give it the lustrous raven-black hue characteristic of many *tsuba*. The background is filled with incredibly fine and accurate punching in the 'fish-roe' technique.

In the centre of the plate is a black lacquer *inrō* or medicine-box with a design in fine gold lacquer of a courtesan, probably based on a colour-print. She is seated with a writing-brush in her hand, wearing the usual pensive look, no doubt pondering a love-letter. Such boxes hung on the end of the sash which went through the belt at the waist and were held at the top by *netsuke*, of which three are shown in the plate. Every material, skill and technique was pressed into their manufacture. *Medicine-boxes*

At the bottom left is a demon mask of red lacquer. The *ōni* or demon plays a large part in Japanese mythology and folklore, and appears in many forms. In the centre is an ivory netsuke, a popular material, with a favourite motif: a horse jumping through a cobweb. In the top left-hand corner is a small round ivory *manju* or bun-shaped button with a design in raised relief of a warrior subduing a demon. Such adjuncts of dress were made in their thousands and absorbed the talents of countless craftsmen-artists in schools spread throughout Japan. The Japanese skill with the chisel is amply illustrated in these miniature works, which provide their many enthusiasts with an endless world of minuscule masterpieces. *Netsuke*

Finally, to complete this survey we must consider some of the vast output of ceramics produced in the Edo period. Unlike those of China, Japanese wares were produced by many different kilns, some large and some small, in various areas of Japan; they were also influenced by individual artists who worked as potters. Thus Japanese ceramics are far more varied and complicated than those in China. Basically the output can be divided into three types: the wares influenced by the seventeenth- and eighteenth-century decorative style seen in paintings of the Sōtatsu–Kōrin school, the tea-ceremony wares and the porcelain influenced by Chinese example. The outstanding name among decorative potters is that of Ninsei, who was active in the mid-seventeenth century. The inspiration for this specimen is essentially Japanese, and comes from the paintings CERAMICS

Ninsei

PLATE P 209

and fine lacquer works for which the Japanese craftsmen have always been renowned. The decorations, often on a black glaze, are in rich enamel colours with a liberal use of gold. In many of these products the decoration is held in balance and, though the effect is purely ornamental, the painterly quality of the decoration carries the weight of the piece. The danger with this type of ware was that the decoration could easily be overdone, as, in fact, frequently occurred. The best examples are models of Japanese taste and careful workmanship. The motifs are such typical Japanese decorative themes as cherry-blossom, wistaria, plum-blossom and pine.

Kenzan

The outstanding potter of the tradition was probably Kenzan (1664–1743), whom we have mentioned as the brother of the painter Kōrin. He ran through a fortune in his gentleman's pottery near Kyōtō and was only rescued from poverty by a patron who brought him to Edo at the age of seventy; here he packed a tremendous activity into his remaining years. His work is very much in the vein of Kōrin, with the accent on simple themes, executed boldly and

FIG. 63
PLATE P. 210

with dashing calligraphy. Kōrin often painted the decoration of his vessels. The ceramic water-container in the form of a wooden bucket is an early piece with waves and water plants on a white background. It was intended for the tea ceremony, as were many of the products of this school.

Kutani ware
PLATE P. 209

Among the earliest in date are the Kutani porcelains made in a village of that name in Kaga prefecture in the second half of the seventeenth century. It is generally assumed that when Hideyoshi returned from his invasion of Korea he brought with him Korean potters who settled in Japan where they could find material suitable for porcelain manufacture. They passed on both their skills and the designs of Chinese Ming and Ch'ing wares. The Old Kutanı wares, especially the green Kutani, have a vivid range of colours in which the bright dark green is characteristic. The decoration is often a combination of rough geometric and bold naturalistic themes which on the somewhat coarse and heavy body create the impression of strength and confidence allied to a bold sense of design.

Arita ware

The remaining two illustrations come from a very large group of porcelain known generically as Arita wares from the name of a site in the southern island of Kyūshū, where large deposits of white porcelain clay were found which led to production in tremendous quantities from the early seventeenth century onwards. The first of these is the Kakiemon group, founded by the first Kakiemon who moved to Arita in about 1615 and is said to have discovered how to produce red overglaze decoration in approximately 1640. However, this probably did not happen until the period between 1660 and 1690. The quality of the white background and brilliant colours is as good as anything produced in the East and even the Chinese imported it. Japanese Kakiemon wares were also the inspiration of Meissen and Chantilly Delft. The plate on page 209 shows a bowl with designs of flowers and birds in a style influenced by the Chinese but typically Japanese in arrangement. The decorations and shapes of these wares exhibit an unlimited variety.

Kakiemon ware
PLATE P. 209

The finest of all Arita wares are of a type known as Nabeshima from the name of a feudal family which acted as patrons of the kiln. These wares were mostly made at Ōkōchi and intended for the use of the family, which took pains to maintain extremely high standards. The underglaze blue with its characteristic soft hue and the over-glaze enamels are always painted with great delicacy on a milky white background, which gives an overall softness to the general appearance. The narrow-waisted vase in the plate on page 209, said to be for ceremonial offerings of wine, is unusual in shape, for most of the surviving Nabeshima is in the form of plates. However, it is typical of the quality and the design that one sees in much of the decorative art of these centuries — notably a tendency to splash a single motif boldly over the whole area rather than to have a repetition of smaller motifs neatly contained in panels or restricted areas. Here the artist has used the traditional 'Three Friends' motif of pine-tree, bamboo and flowering plum in a palette of red, yellow and purple; on the other side of the vase are an orange, cranes and tortoises. This vase epitomizes the quality and decorative skill which the Japanese potters rapidly acquired and which made their products not only the wonder of Europe but even highly sought after in China, the home of porcelain.

Nabeshima ware
PLATE P. 209

PLATE P. 209

The decline and fall of the Tokugawa rulers were due to many diverse

FALL OF
TOKUGAWA

factors. They were quite unable to manage or even understand the complications of their expanding economy. Inflation and debased currency constantly harried them. The recurring periods of bad harvests led to widespread agrarian risings which they controlled only with the greatest difficulty. The local lords found themselves heavily in debt, mostly to the rich merchants, and quite incapable of ordering their finances. The rulers themselves were of a very different calibre from the founders of the régime.

The intelligent members of society were very conscious of the changes taking place in the outside world and anxious to share in them. The whole atmosphere of the body politic was diseased, with nobody knowing enough or being strong enough to cure the sickness. The third factor was the expanding commercial and imperially-minded nations of Europe and America. Only for a time could Japan resist the forces knocking on her door and it was the United *Isolation policy* States which finally forced her to abandon her isolationist policy and *abandoned* allow foreigners into the country. Under the leadership of a number of powerful lords, such as Satsuma and Chōshū, the enfeebled Tokugawa generalissimos were quietly toppled and, using the emperor as a rallying point, they restored the throne to power and introduced a parliamentary system of government. With this Japan entered the modern world and in a remarkably short time was able to rid herself of any traces of incipient colonialism, westernize her economy and armed forces, and take her place as a fully independent, powerful nation; less than one hundred years later she was able to challenge the United States and the British Commonwealth. Immediately following the opening of the country, the Japanese tended to accept everything Western without discrimination. Western art styles had a tremendous vogue and Western-style art schools were opened. After little more than a decade, inspired by Western scholars like Fenollosa, Japan turned once more to the preservation of her past. Museums were founded and surveys initiated to protect the nation's treasures. To the latter we owe many of the masterpieces illustrated in this book.

Meanwhile Japanese artists were travelling to Europe and both learning from and contributing to the Parisian world of art. The

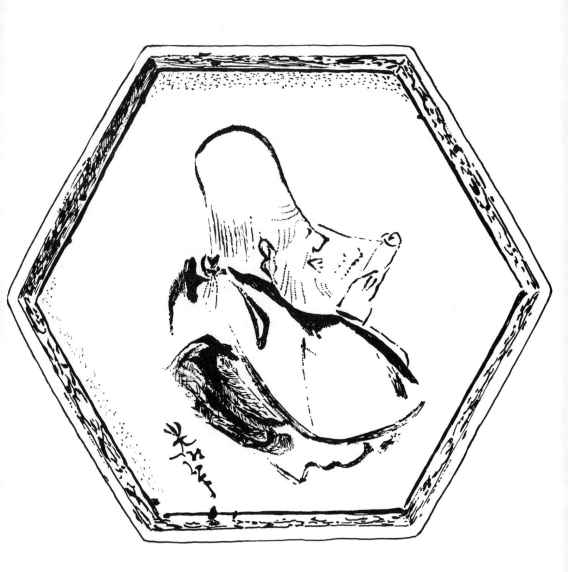

FIG. 62 – *Hexagonal dish by Kenzan, decorated in ink by Kōrin. Diameter 27 cm. K. Ōkura Collection, Tokyo. Cf. p. 197. 220·*

Japanese skill with the brush was a revelation to Europe, as were the Japanese craft products that were shown in the trade fairs and exhibitions. Japanese painters obtained inspiration from every source they contacted. More recently the West, too, has learned from Japanese calligraphy and craft design. Our potters are as deeply indebted to them as they are to China. Modern prints are highly sought after.

Of course, Japan is now fully in the stream of international movements in modern art and contributes to them as much as she borrows. What is created one week in Tokyo can be seen the next in New York. Artistically this is an exciting age, but it would take another volume to explore all the complications and ramifications of the myriad movements that exist in Japan, whose people have an artistic energy which seems truly inexhaustible.

APPENDICES

CHRONOLOGICAL TABLE

JAPAN	CHINA	KOREA
B.C.	481–221	
1000 to *c.* 200 B.C.	WARRING STATES	
JŌMON PERIOD	(late Chou period)	
300 '*Cord-pattern' pottery, dogū*		
figures		
200 *c.* 200 B.C.–A.D. 500	221–206	
YAYOI PERIOD	CH'IN DYNASTY	
Potter's wheel		
100	206 B.C.–A.D. 220	108 B.C.–A.D. 313
	HAN DYNASTY	Nang-Nang (Lo-lang,
		Rakurō); Han colony
A.D.	65 first evidence of Buddhist	1st cent. B.C. ?–668 Koguryo
100	communities	1st cent. B.C. ?–663 Paekche
200	220–265	1st cent. B.C. ?–668 Silla
	THREE EMPIRES	
300 300–*c.* 700	265–581	
TUMULUS PERIOD	SIX DYNASTIES	372 Koguryo becomes
Haji and Sue ware; haniwa	3rd–4th cents. spread of Buddhism	Buddhist
	in North and South China	
	Earliest extant Buddhist figure,	
	partly under influence of	384 Paekche becomes
	Gandhāra	Buddhist
400 Earliest cultural influences	386–535	424–524 Silla becomes
from China and Korea (incl.	NORTHERN WEI DYNASTY	Buddhist
writing)	445–6 persecution of Buddhists	
500	5th–6th cents. *cave-temples of Yün-*	
	kang, Lung-mên	
	c. 500 Ch'an Buddhism	
552 Buddhism adopted from	reaches China	
Paekche (official date)	550–581	
	NORTHERN CH'I / NORTHERN	
538–645	CHOU DYNASTY	6th–7th cents. *flowering period*
ASUKA (SUIKO) PERIOD	*Caves of Hsiang-t'ang-shan*	*of early Buddhist art*
574–622 Crown Prince Shōtoku	Late 6th cent. *T'ien-t'ai school*	
Art under Korean influence		
600 607 *Hōryū-ji Temple founded*	581–618	
623 *Shaka Triad by Tori*	SUI DYNASTY	
645 Taika reform	618–906	
	T'ANG DYNASTY	
	Capital: Ch'ang-an	
700 645–712		668–935
HAKUHŌ PERIOD		Kingdoms united in
Art under Sui and early T'ang		GREATER SILLA EMPIRE
influence. Tamamushi shrine	*Wu Tao-tzu, painter*	Capital: Kyongju

226

CHRONOLOGICAL TABLE

	JAPAN	CHINA	KOREA
A.D.			
	710–784 NARA PERIOD *Buddhist art modelled* *on that of T'ang* Capital: Nara (*Yakushi-ji* *Temple, Tōdai-ji Temple, etc.*) 752 *colossal Buddha* *Wall-painting in Hōryū-ji Temple* *c. 763 Statue of the priest Ganjin*	*Late phase of T'ien-lung-shan* *caves*	7th–9th cents. *classical* *Buddhist art under T'ang* *influence*
800	794–876 EARLY HEIAN PERIOD 810–823 KŌNIN PERIOD 859–876 JŌGAN PERIOD Capital: Heian (=Kyōtō) *Monasteries on Hiei-zan (Tendai* *school) and Kōyasan (Shingon* *school); syncretism of* *Buddhism and Shintō*	843–5 persecution of Buddhists Ennin, Japanese monk, in China	
900	895–1185 FUJIWARA (LATE HEIAN) PERIOD Flowering of courtly culture, largely independent of China and Korea *Red Fudō*	906–960 FIVE DYNASTIES 960–1278 SUNG DYNASTY NORTHERN SUNG 960—1127 LIAO DYNASTY 907–1125	932–1392 Koryo period Capital: Kaesong *Continuation of Silla art;* *some Sung influence*
1000	*Chōjū Giga* *Shigisan-engi-emaki*		1097 Ch'an (Son) Buddhism spreads to Korea
1100	*Genji-monogatari-emaki* 1185–1392 KAMAKURA PERIOD Kamakura headquarters of military rulers Feudal warrior culture *Portrait of Minamoto Yoritomo*	SOUTHERN SUNG 1127–1278	
1200	Zen Buddhism introduced *Monasteries at Kamakura* Further Chinese influence (Sung) *Sculpture: Unkei and his school* 1252 *colossal Buddha at* *Kamakura*	*Ch'an Buddhist ink-painting* (esp. 13th c.) Neo-Confucianism	1269–1280 Mongol invasions
1300	Tengū-sōshi *Ippen-shōnin-emaki* 1338–1573 ASHIKAGA (MUROMACHI) PERIOD	1278–1368 YÜAN (Mongol) DYNASTY Lamaism makes headway, esp. in North China	

227

CHRONOLOGICAL TABLE

JAPAN	CHINA	KOREA

A.D.

Tosa school
Flowering of Zen art
(ink-painting, tea ceremony)
in Kyōtō under strong Chinese
influence
c. 1345 *ink-painting*
'*Kanzan*' *by Kaō*
1389 *Kinkaku-ji Temple*

1368–1644
MING DYNASTY
Paintings in the 'literary man's
style' (wên-jên)

1392–1910
YI DYNASTY
Confucianism; decline of
Buddhism *and Buddhist art*

1400   1420–1506 *Sesshū*
Kanō school

1500   1539–1610 *Hasegawa Tōhaku*
1568–1615
MOMOYAMA PERIOD
1583 *Portrait of Oda Nobunaga*
1583–1585 Hideyoshi builds
Ōsaka castle
c. 1600 *Namban-byōbu*

1600   1615–1868
TOKUGAWA (Edo) PERIOD
Seat of rulers (shōguns)
at Edo (= Tokyo)
1602 Ieyasu builds
Nijō castle
1558?–1632 *Kōetsu*
Early 17th cent. *Sōtatsu*
1658–1716 *Kōrin*
1664–1743 *Kenzan*
Late phase of Zen
painting (Zen-ga)

1644–1912
CH'ING DYNASTY

1700   1688–1703 Genroku era
Ukiyo-e
1753/4–1806 *Utamarō*
c. 1794–1795 (active) *Sharaku*
1760–1849 *Hokusai*

1800   1797–1858 *Hiroshige*

BIBLIOGRAPHY

Armbruster, Gisela, Das Shigisan-Engi-Emaki (Heidelberg 1958).

Baltzer, F., Die Architektur der Kultbauten Japans (Berlin 1907).

Berlin, Staatliche Museen, Ausstellung altjapanischer Kunst (Berlin 1939).

Bersihand, Roger, Geschichte Japans (Stuttgart 1963).

Binyon, Robert Laurence, Painting in the Far East (3rd rev. ed., London–New York 1960).

Binyon, Robert Laurence and Sexton, J. J. O'Brien, Japanese Colour Prints (ed. by B. Gray, 2nd ed., London 1960).

Blaser, Werner, Tempel und Teehaus in Japan (Olten-Lausanne 1955).

Blaser, Werner, Wohnen und Bauen in Japan (Teufen, Aargau 1958).

Boller, Willy, Meister des japanischen Farbholzschnitts (Berne 1947).

Bowers, Faubion, Japanese Theatre (London 1954).

Brasch, Kurt, Hakuin und die Zen-Malerei (Tokyo 1957).

Brasch, Kurt, Zenga (Tokyo 1961).

Brower, Robert H. and Miner, Earl, Japanese Court Poetry (Stanford, Calif. 1961).

Buhot, J., Histoire des arts du Japon (vol.I, Paris 1949).

Conze, E., Buddhism (Oxford 1951).

Drexler, A., The Architecture of Japan (New York 1955).

Eliot, Sir Charles N. E., Japanese Buddhism (London 1959).

Feddersen, Martin, Japanisches Kunstgewerbe (Brunswick 1960).

Feddersen, Martin, Das Kunstgewerbe Ostasiens, in: Bosserts Geschichte des Kunstgewerbes aller Zeiten und Völker, vol. III (Berlin 1930).

Fischer, Otto, Die Kunst Indiens, Chinas und Japans (Propyläen-Kunstgeschichte, Berlin 1928).

Glaser, Curt, Die Kunst Ostasiens (Leipzig 1913; 2nd ed., 1920).

Gray, Basil, Japanese Screen Painting (London 1955).

Grilli, Elise, Golden Screen Paintings of Japan (London 1961).

Grilli, Elise, Sharaku (London 1959).

Grilli, Elise, Japanese Picture Scrolls (London 1959).

Grousset, René, The Civilizations of the East (Vol. IV, Japan; 4 vols., London–New York 1931–4).

Gunsaulus, Helen C., The Clarence Buckingham Collection of Japanese Prints: the Primitives (Chicago 1955).

Gunsaulus, Helen C., Japanese Textiles (The Japan Society of New York 1941).

Harada, Jiro, A Glimpse of Japanese Ideals (Tokyo 1937).

Harada, Y., English Catalogue of Treasures in the Imperial Repository Shōsōin (Tokyo 1932).

Hasumi, T., Japanische Plastik (Fribourg 1960).

Hempel, Rose, Zenga. Malerei des Zen-Buddhismus (Munich 1960).

Hillier, J. R., The Japanese Print: a New Approach (London 1960).

Hillier, J. R., Hokusai (London 1955).

Hillier, J. R., Japanese Masters of the Colour Print (London 1954).

Hillier, J. R., Utamaro, Colour Prints and Paintings (London 1961).

Hisamatsu, Shin'ichi, Zen to bijutsu (Zen and Fine Arts; Kyoto 1958).

Honey, William Bowyer, Ceramic Art of China and other Countries of the Far East (London 1949).

Ishida, M. and Wada, G., The Shōsōin: an 8th-Century Treasure House (Tokyo 1954).

Iwamiya, Takeji, Schönheit japanischer Formen (Fribourg 1964).

Iwamiya, Takeji, Geheimnis japanischer Schönheit (Fribourg 1965).

Jakobsen, Kristian, Japanische Teekeramik (Brunswick 1958).

Japan: Ancient Buddhist Paintings. Preface by S. Elisséeff. Introd. by T. Matsushita. (UNESCO World Art Series, No. 11, Greenwich, Conn., 1949).

Japan: the Official Guide (Tokyo 1962).

Jenyns, Soame, Japanese Porcelain (London 1965).

Jenyns, Soame, The Wares of Kutani, in: Transactions of the Oriental Ceramic Society, vol. XXI (1945–6).

Joly, H. L., Japanese Sword-Mounts (London 1910).

Kidder, J. E., Japan before Buddhism (London 1959).

Kidder, J. E., Early Japanese Art (London 1964).

Kidder, J. E., The Jōmon Pottery of Japan (Ascona 1957).

Kidder, J. E., Masterpieces of Japanese sculpture (Rutland, Vt., 1961).

Kikuchi, Sadao, Hokusai (Tokyo 1956).

Kikuchi, Sadao, Hokusai. With an introduction and notes by P. C. Swann (London 1959).

Kobayashi, Takeshi, Study on Life and Works of Unkei (Okajima 1954).

Kondo, Ichitaro, Kitagawa Utamaro. English adaptation by C. S. Terry (Tokyo 1957).

Kōrin-ha Gashū (Masterpieces Selected from the Kōrin School), 5 vols. (Tokyo 1903–6).

Koyama, Fujio and Figgess, John, Two Thousand Years of Oriental Ceramics (New York 1961).

Kultermann, Udo, Neues Bauen in Japan (Tübingen 1960).

Kümmel, Otto, Die Kunst Chinas, Japans und Koreas (Handbuch der Kunstwissenschaft; Wildpark-Potsdam 1929).

Kuno, T., A Guide to Japanese Sculpture (Tokyo 1963).

Kyoto National Museum: Muromachi jidai shoga (Painting and Calligraphy of Muromachi Period) (Special Exhibition April 27–May 8, 1961; Kyoto 1961).

Ledoux, Louis Vernon, Japanese Prints of the Primitive Period in the Collection of Louis V. Ledoux (New York 1942).

Ledoux, Louis Vernon, Japanese Prints, Bunchō to Utamaro, in the Collection of Louis V. Ledoux (New York 1948).

Ledoux, Louis Vernon, Japanese Prints, Harunobu and Shunshō, in the Collection of Louis V. Ledoux (New York 1945).

Ledoux, Louis Vernon, Japanese Prints, Hokusai and Hiroshige, in the Collection of Louis V. Ledoux (Princeton 1951).

Ledoux, Louis Vernon, Japanese Prints, Sharaku to Toyokuni, in the Collection of Louis V. Ledoux (Princeton 1950).

Lee, Sherman E., Tea Taste in Japanese Art (New York 1963).

Lee, Sherman E., A History of Far Eastern Art (London 1964).

Meinertzhagen, F., The Art of the Netsuke Carver (London 1956).

Michener, James A., The Floating World (London 1955; New York 1954).

Michener, James A., Japanese Prints from the Early Masters to the Modern (Rutland, Vt. 1959).

Minamoto, H., An Illustrated History of Japanese Art (Kyoto 1935).

Mitsuoka, T., Ceramic Art of Japan (4th rev. ed., Tokyo 1956).

Miller, Roy Andrew, Japanese Ceramics (after the Japanese text by Seiichi Okuda, Fujio Koyama and Seizo Hayashiya; Rutland, Vt. 1960; New York 1962).

Moriya, Kenji, Die japanische Malerei (Wiesbaden 1953).

Munsterberg, Hugo, Landscape Painting of China and Japan (Tokyo 1956).

Munsterberg, Hugo, The Arts of Japan (Tokyo–London 1957; Rutland, Vt. 1962).

Murasaki, Shikibu, The Tale of Genji. Trans. by Arthur Waley, 6 vols. (London 1925–33).

Nabeshima House Factory Research Committee, Nabeshima Coloured Porcelains (Kyoto 1954).

Naitō, Tōichirō, The Wall Paintings of Hōryū-ji (Baltimore 1943).

Nakamura, Keidan, Eitoku. (Japanese Famous Painting, Series 1, Tokyo 1957?).

Nihon Emakimono Shūsei (Collection of Japanese Picture Scrolls), 22 vols. Japanese text by Tanaka Ichimatsu (Tokyo 1929–32).

Nihon Emakimono Zenshū (Japanese Scroll Paintings), 15 vols. (Tokyo 1958-).

Nippon Seikwa (Art Treasures of Japan), 5 vols. (Nara 1908–11).

Nishimura, Tei, Namban Art: Christian Art in Japan, 1549-1639 (Tokyo 1958).

Noma, Seiroku and Kuno, Takeshi, Albums of Japanese Sculpture, 6 vols. (Tokyo 1953).

Noma, Seiroku, The Arts of Japan, Ancient and Medieval. Translated and adapted by John Rosenfield (Tokyo 1965).

Oakland Art Museum, Japanese Ceramics from Ancient to Modern Times, Selected from Collections in Japan and America. (February 4–26, 1961; ed. by Fujio Koyama, Oakland, Calif. 1961).

Okamoto, Yoshitomo, Namban Byōbuko (A Study of Folding Screens Depicting the Westerners Coming to Japan through the Southern Islands; Tokyo 1955).

Old Imari Research Committee (ed.): Old Imari (Tokyo 1959).

Paine, Robert T., Japanese Screen Painting (Boston 1935).

Paine, Robert T. and Soper, Alexander C., The Art and Architecture of Japan. (Pelican History of Art; Harmondsworth 1955; 2nd ed., 1960).

Sammlung Tony Straus-Negbauer. Japanische

Farbenholzschnitte des 17.–19. Jahrhunderts (Berlin 1928).
Sansom, Sir George Bailey, Japan: a Short Cultural History (London 1931; rev. ed., 1946).
Sansom, Sir George Bailey, A History of Japan, 3 vols. (London 1959).
Seckel, Dietrich, Das älteste Langrollenbild in Japan: Kako-Genzai-Ingakyō, in: Bulletin of Eastern Art, no. 37 (Tokyo 1943).
Seckel, Dietrich, The Art of Buddhism (ART OF THE WORLD Series). Translated by A. E. Keep (London 1964).
Seckel, Dietrich, Buddhistische Kunst Ostasiens (Stuttgart 1957).
Seckel, Dietrich, Emakimono: the Art of the Japanese Painted Hand-scroll. Photographs and foreword by Akihisa Hasé. Translated by J. M. Brownjohn (New York 1959).
Seckel, Dietrich, Einführung in die Kunst Ostasiens (Munich 1960).
Seidlitz, Woldemar von, A History of Japanese Colour-Prints (London 1910).
Sekai Toji Zenshū (Catalogue of World's Ceramics), 16 vols. (Tokyo 1955–6).
Smith, Bradley, Japan: a History in Art (1964).
Society of Friends of Eastern Art: Index of Japanese Painters (Tokyo 1959).
Soper, Alexander C., The Rise of Yamato-e, in: Art Bulletin, vol. XXIV (December 1942).
Soper, Alexander C., Illustrative Method of the Tokugawa Genji Pictures, in: Art Bulletin, vol. XXXVII (March 1955).
Soper, Alexander C., The Evolution of Buddhist Architecture in Japan (Princeton 1942).
Sōtatsu Kōrin Byōga-shū (Collection of Screen Paintings by Sōtatsu and Kōrin; 3rd ed., Kyoto 1919).
Speiser, Werner, Die Kunst Ostasiens (Berlin 1946; reprint, 1956).
Speiser, Werner, Chinesische und japanische Malerei, in: Meisterwerke aussereuropäischer Malerei (Berlin 1959).
Stewart, Basil, Subjects Portrayed in Japanese Colour-Prints (London 1922).
Strange, E. F., Japanese Colour Prints (London 1931).
Suzuki, Susumu, Buson (Japanese Famous Painting, Series 1; Tokyo 1956).
Suzuki, Susumu and others, Ike-no Taiga sakuhin shū (The Works of Ike-no Taiga), 2 vols. (Tokyo 1960).

Suzuki, Tokashi, Hiroshige (New York 1958).
Swann, Peter C., An Introduction to the Arts of Japan (Oxford 1958).
Swann, Peter C., Hokusai (London 1959).
Tajima, Shiichi (ed.), Kōrin-ha Gwashū (A Collection of Drawings by Kōrin and his School; 1903).
Takahashi, Sei-Ichiro, The Evolution of Ukiyo-e: the Artistic, Economic and Social Significance of Japanese Wood-block Prints (Yokohama 1955).
Taki, Seiichi, Three Essays on Oriental Painting (London 1910).
Tanaka, Sakutaro, Ninsei (Wares by Ninsei). Tōki Zenshū, no. 24 (Tokyo 1960).
Toda, Kenji, Japanese Scroll Painting (Chicago 1935).
Tōki Zenshū (Ceramic Series: Collective Catalogue of Pottery and Porcelain of Different Periods in Japan, China and Korea), 28 vols. (Tokyo 1957).
Tokyo National Museum, Pageant of Japanese Art, 6 vols. (Tokyo 1952–).
Tokyo National Museum, Exhibition of Japanese Buddhist Arts (Tokyo 1956).
Tsudzumi, Tsuneyoshi, Die Kunst Japans (Leipzig 1929).
Volker, T., The Japanese Porcelain Trade of the Dutch East India Company after 1683 (Leyden 1959).
Warner, Langdon, The Craft of the Japanese Sculptor (New York 1936).
Warner, Langdon, The Enduring Art of Japan (Cambridge, Mass. 1952).
Warner, Langdon, Japanese Sculpture of the Tempyō Period (Cambridge, Mass. 1964).
Watson, W., Sculpture of Japan (London 1959).
Yashiro, Yukio, Two Thousand Years of Japanese Art. Edited by Peter C. Swann and others (London 1958).
Yashiro, Yukio, Art Treasures of Japan, 2 vols. (Tokyo 1960).
Yoshida, Tetsurō, Japanische Architektur (Tübingen 1952).
Yoshida, Tetsurō, The Japanese House and Garden. Translated by Marcus G. Sims (London 1955).
Yoshida, Tetsurō, Gardens of Japan. Translated by Marcus G. Sims (London 1957).
Yoshizawa, Chu, Taiga. (Japanese Famous Painting, Series 1, Tokyo 1957).

INDEX